IMAGES
of Aviation

INDIANOLA
BALLOONING CAPITAL OF IOWA

IMAGES
of Aviation

INDIANOLA
BALLOONING CAPITAL OF IOWA

Dennis D. Nicholson and Becky S. Wigeland

ARCADIA
PUBLISHING

Published by Arcadia Publishing
Charleston SC, Chicago IL, Portsmouth NH, San Francisco CA

Library of Congress Control Number: 2009938222

For all general information contact Arcadia Publishing at:
Telephone 843-853-2070
Fax 843-853-0044
E-mail sales@arcadiapublishing.com
For customer service and orders:
Toll-Free 1-888-313-2665

Visit us on the Internet at www.arcadiapublishing.com

*This book is dedicated to all the men and women who had the curiosity
and daring to explore, invent, and become the first ones to fly.
They gave their all, and sometimes their lives, to make the dream the
reality it is today, more than 200 years after the first flight in 1783.
In particular, we dedicate this book to the ballooning
pioneers who brought the sport of ballooning to Iowa and
Indianola, and to the thousands of volunteers who have kept
the adventure of ballooning alive and growing here.
We dedicate it also to those who had the dream and the
tenacity to establish the National Balloon Museum in order
to tell the story of the adventure for all generations.
Many of them are named in this book, but we could not name
them all. However, they made it possible today for countless
thousands to enjoy what has been called the "sport of the gods."
This is their story, and it could not have been written without them.
Enjoy the book, and catch the fever!*

CONTENTS

Acknowledgments   6

Introduction   7

1.   First Iowa Balloon Flights   9

2.   Early Beginnings   15

3.   Ballooning for the Masses   25

4.   Sport Ballooning Comes of Age in the 1960s   29

5.   Sport Ballooning Comes to Indianola   43

6.   Ballooning Spreads across Iowa   59

7.   Ballooning in Indianola Evolves   69

8.   Indianola Becomes Site of the National Balloon Museum   73

9.   Ballooning over Indianola Fascinates the Crowds   117

10. Color Photo Album   129

ACKNOWLEDGMENTS

Grateful acknowledgment is made to the following persons who helped us gather information or with research for facts and photographs (in alphabetical order):

Anderson-Abruzzo-Albuquerque International Balloon Museum.
Tracy Barnes, ballooning pioneer, former balloon manufacturer and 2008 hall of fame.
Jürgen Bleibler and Barbara Waibel, Luftschiffbau Zeppelin GMbH.
Arlan Brown, early volunteer and current crew coordinator for National Balloon Classic.
Mary Conklin, volunteer for ballooning, scorekeeper and museum board secretary.
Kory Darnall, Schuezenpark Gilde, Davenport, Iowa.
Robert Fiedler, reference librarian, Musser Public Library, Muscatine, Iowa.
Phillip Gray, local balloonist and balloon manufacturer.
Becky Kakac, current office secretary of the National Balloon Classic.
Blair Lawson, balloonist and current museum volunteer.
Tim McConnell, local balloonist and photographer for photographic research.
Tom McConnell, ballooning pioneer and ballooning historian
Greg Marchant, current executive director of the National Balloon Classic.
National Balloon Museum Auxiliary members who assisted with proofing or research.
National Museum of the U.S. Air Force.
Orvin Olivier, balloonist and former Balloon Federation of America board member.
The photographers who provided pictures to tell the story. (See credits on each picture.)
Don Piccard, ballooning pioneer and former balloon manufacturer.
Matthew T. Reitzel, archivist—state archives, South Dakota State Historical Society.
Sharon Ripperger, office manager of the Balloon Federation of America.
Gary Ruble, key organizer for ballooning, balloonist, and a museum board member.
Bob Shelton, current president of Iowa Balloonists Association.
Eugene T. "Gene" Smith, early volunteer, museum officer, treasurer, and museum historian.
Marlene Wall, a leader in the ballooning movement and the museum for many years.
Jim Weinman, active in helping organize ballooning events and establish the museum.
Maxine Weinman, who for many years was museum curator.
Dave Wesner, ballooning historian and current a member of the museum board.
James W. "Jim" Winker, ballooning pioneer, ballooning historian, and 2009 hall of fame.
Mme. Zerkane, Bibliothèque nationale de France (National Library of France).

A special thank-you to the following people who read the entire text and provided their knowledge to ensure the accuracy of the story and grammatical integrity: Jim and Maxine Weinman, Gary Ruble, Marlene Wall, Nancy Griffin, and Amy Duncan.

INTRODUCTION

This is the story of ballooning in Iowa but, in particular, the story of ballooning in Indianola, Iowa, which is now known as the ballooning capital of Iowa. The first balloon flight in Iowa occurred on October 9, 1856, in Muscatine, Iowa. The records of early balloon flights in the Indianola area are sparse, but there were occasional exhibition flights of gas balloons at the Warren County Fair in Indianola in the early 1900s.

To put Iowa balloon flights in perspective, one must look at early aviation history of both the balloon and the fixed-wing aircraft. The first time anyone flew in a hot air balloon was in Paris, France, on November 21, 1783. There was no dependable heat source for that first balloon, so it was not practical for flying. Just 10 days after that flight, a hydrogen gas–filled balloon was launched in Paris. Gas ballooning was more dependable, so the efforts for flying then focused on gas balloons.

By the 1900s, gas-filled airships began to be built. They were equipped with internal combustion engines and propellers, which made it possible to control direction and speed.

Following the first flight of a fixed-wing aircraft by the Wright brothers in 1903, the fixed-wing aircraft developed in parallel with airship development, and in 1927, Charles Lindberg made his famous nonstop flight from New York to Paris in his plane called the *Spirit of St. Louis*.

The most famous of the great airships was the Hindenburg, built in Germany in 1936. The danger of using hydrogen gas eventually caused the demise of the great airships, and as fixed-wing aircraft developed, they gradually replaced the airships. While the airships were carrying passengers, scientists were using teardrop-shaped gas balloons for exploring the stratosphere and gathering scientific data.

Ballooning for the masses would have to wait until the invention of the modern hot air balloon at Raven Industries in South Dakota by Iowa-born Paul E. "Ed" Yost in 1960. Yost invented a new propane gas burner that provided a practical heat source and a new balloon envelope. With the new technology, it did not take long for hot air ballooning to become a sport for the masses. Balloonists Ed Yost and Don Piccard in April 1963 made the first flight of the modern hot air balloon across the English Channel. In the 1960s and early 1970s balloon-manufacturing companies were started. Balloon clubs and ballooning events sprang up, and people began to enjoy the new sport of ballooning during the mid- to late 1960s, 1970s, and beyond.

In 1970, the U.S. National Hot Air Balloon Championships came to Indianola, Iowa. The success of the 1970 nationals held in Indianola led the Balloon Federation of America (BFA) to choose Indianola to host the national championships for 18 consecutive years.

Many other ballooning events were spawned all across Iowa, but Indianola remains the primary center of ballooning in Iowa. Ballooning in Iowa is supported by two balloon clubs, one balloon manufacturer, and three balloon repair stations. It is not uncommon to see hot air balloons flying in the Indianola area in early morning or evening any time of the year.

When the National Hot Air Balloon Championship moved to other locations in 1989, the National Balloon Classic was established and continues to keep the tradition of ballooning alive in Indianola.

When the idea of building a National Ballooning Museum was born, it was only natural that Indianola would become the site for it, due to its close association with the U.S. National Hot Air Balloon Championships for so many years. As early as 1972, informal ballooning exhibits were temporarily displayed during the U.S. nationals. By 1973, the BFA decided to promote the building of a balloon museum. Museum exhibits were housed in a variety of locations around the city until the museum building was finally opened in 1988. Not only is Indianola the ballooning capital of Iowa, but the location of the museum there makes Indianola the repository of ballooning history for the nation.

The presence here of the National Balloon Museum and the U.S. Ballooning Hall of Fame together with the annual nine-day National Balloon Classic and the national offices of the Balloon Federation of America draw thousands of visitors each year to Indianola. Not only is Indianola the ballooning capital of Iowa, but it could almost be called the ballooning capital of the United States, or at least of the Midwest.

One

First Iowa

Balloon Flights

Early balloon flights in Iowa and Indianola were hydrogen-filled gas balloons. It was most common for these flights to be made at public events such as county fairs. These flights included both basic round-shaped balloons as well as oblong-shaped, gas-filled airships with motors and propellers to control flight direction and speed of movement. Many of the flights also included people jumping out of the aircraft and parachuting down to the crowds of spectators below. These events were not everyday occurrences as the process of producing the hydrogen and filling the balloon was a somewhat complicated and time consuming activity.

Since the beginning of time, human beings have wanted to emulate the birds and glide above the Earth. In Iowa, the dream was first realized on October 9, 1856, in southeast Iowa with the use of a hydrogen-filled gas balloon. The flight was arranged by aeronautic professor Silas Brooks. His assistant, a young man by the name of John Leonard, was the pilot. The flight began in the courthouse square in Muscatine and traveled approximately 15 miles to a landing 3 miles north of Wilton in Cedar County. Since cameras were not available in 1856, there were no photographs to record the event, but the balloon would have probably looked something like the one in the image above made by an unidentified artist. (Photograph courtesy of the National Balloon Museum Archives.)

There were other early balloon flights made in Iowa after Silas Brooks' assistant, John Leonard, made his flight. One of those was this gas balloon above in Emmetsburg, Iowa, in 1910. It is known that at least the following early balloon flights occurred in Iowa as well: H. W. Durrell in Des Moines in 1867, H. N. Drake in Oskaloosa in 1879, Samuel Baldwin in Keokuk in 1887, William E. Winterringer in Sioux City in 1888, Louisa Bates in Burlington in 1888, a man named Streif in Dubuque in 1889, G. A. Thompson in Dubuque in 1889, someone named Stewart in Burlington in 1890, J. B. Dearing in Sioux City in 1898, and Dorothy de Vonda somewhere in Iowa—location unknown—but prior to 1900. (Photograph courtesy of the National Balloon Museum Archives.)

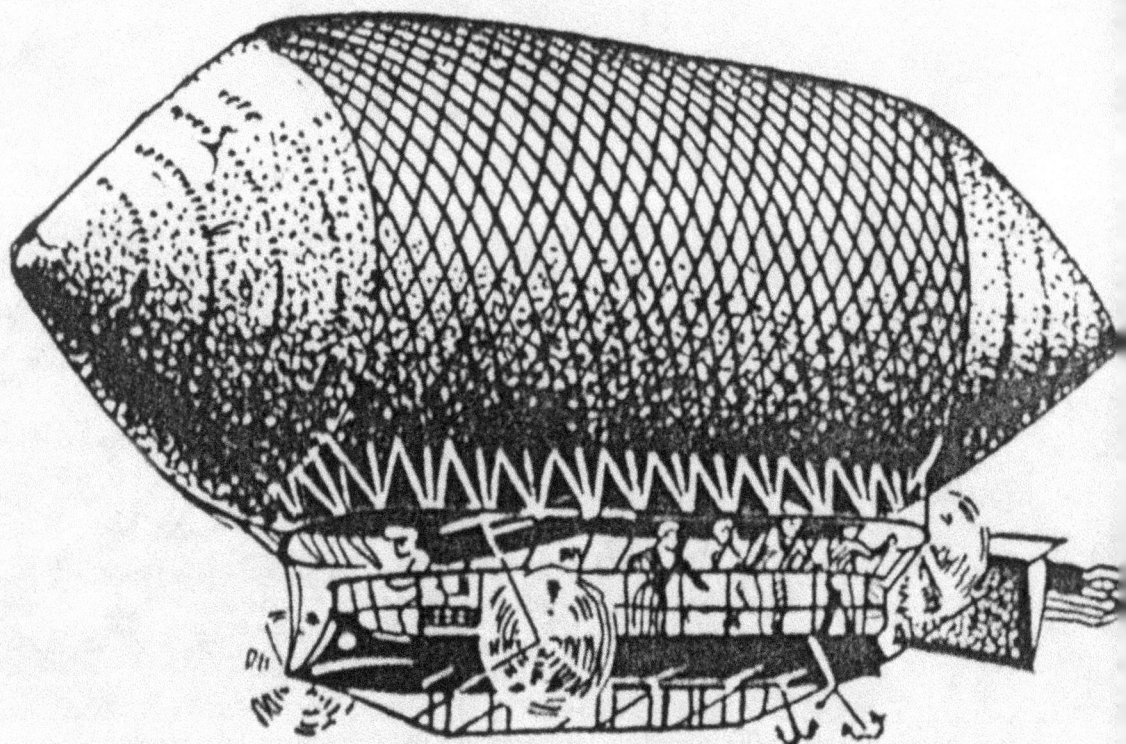

It is believed that a number of gas balloons appeared in Indianola in the early 1900s, but the records are very sparse. The earliest verifiable date was in 1903, when the Pawnee Bill's Wild West and Great Far East show came to the Warren County Fair. They used a gas-filled airship with propellers to control their flight. They made two daily ascensions before the crowds. In addition, they had an equestrian exhibition and a cast of characters who depicted oriental and Wild West Indian stories. (Photograph courtesy of the *Advocate Tribune*.)

It is known that Lucielle Belmont of the famous Belmont Sisters made an appearance at the Warren County Fair in Indianola in the early 1900s, but the date is unknown. Her aerial act involved jumping from the balloon and parachuting down. The ballooning performances in those days were a far cry from the colorful extravagances observed today with multiple colorful hot air balloons. It was not a simple matter to inflate a hydrogen-filled balloon. Equipment had to be brought in to manufacture the gas with a process using iron filings, water, and sulfuric acid. In the process, heat was generated, so the gas also had to be cooled. Otherwise, if the balloon was filled with hot gas, it would leave the balloon only partly inflated when it cooled. It took some time to do all of that. In the case of the first balloon flight in Iowa at Muscatine, the materials and apparatus were brought in two days before the flight. William E. Winterringer made an ascension in this smoke balloon (below) and a parachute jump at the Warren County Fair in 1936. (Photographs courtesy of the National Balloon Museum Archives.)

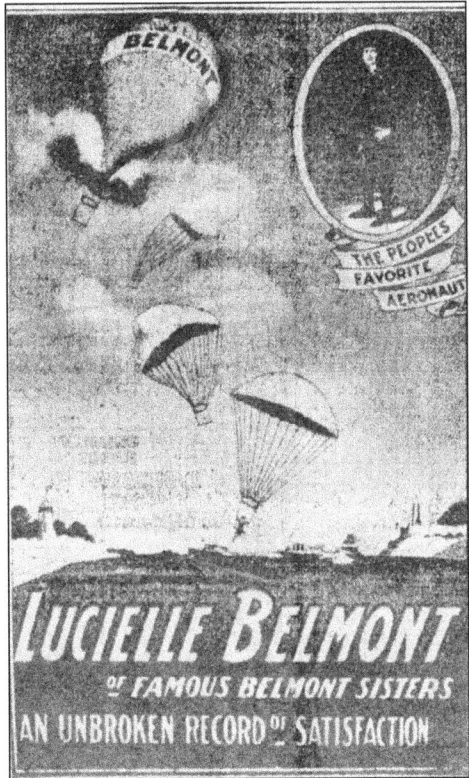

LUCIELLE BELMONT
OF FAMOUS BELMONT SISTERS
AN UNBROKEN RECORD OF SATISFACTION

THE GRAF ZEPPELIN OVER DAVENPORT AUGUST 28, 1929
PHOTO BY A.E. WILLIAMS DAVENPORT TIMES STAFF PHOTOGRAPHER

One of those Iowa flights was made by the Graf Zeppelin airship over Davenport, Iowa, in 1929, which is shown above. It is hard to find records of these early flights, which took place prior to 1900 or the early part of the 20th century primarily because only professional photographers had cameras and taking pictures was still a laborious task. Cameras practical enough for the average person did not come on the scene until around 1900. The above photograph was taken by A. E. Williams, who at the time was a staff photographer for the *Davenport Times* newspaper. (Photograph courtesy of Schutzenpark Gilde of Davenport, Iowa.)

14

Two

EARLY BEGINNINGS

To put modern ballooning into perspective, one must take a look back at the first balloon flights, which occurred in France in 1783. When the first flight took place that year it was a hot air balloon, but with no dependable heat source, the technology was not practical. Because the first gas-filled balloon flight came only a few days after the first hot air balloon flight, and because it provided a more dependable and longer lasting ability to stay aloft, balloon flight was limited to gas balloons until the invention of the modern hot air balloon and propane burner system in the United States in 1960. Beginning in the early 1900s, great airships or dirigibles became the first commercial passenger-carrying aircraft. Concurrently with this development, the Wright brothers' first airplane flight in 1903 started the development of the fixed-wing aircraft as a practical alternative to airships. After the tragic demise of the Hindenburg airship in 1937, airships gradually were replaced by fixed-wing aircraft.

The first balloon flight was made in Paris, France, on November 21, 1783, using a balloon made of paper and silk built by papermakers Joseph and Etienne Montgolfier of Annonay, France. It was piloted by Pilâtre de Rozier and François Laurent Marquis d'Arlandes. That flight lasted about 25 minutes, travelling about 5.5 miles before their meager fuel supply ran out and the balloon cooled off and brought the two men back to earth. There was no dependable heat source for that first hot air balloon, which meant only very short flights were possible. (Photograph courtesy of Bibliothèque nationale de France.)

On December 21, 1783, the first gas balloon flight was launched by Jacques Alexander Charles and Nicholas Louis Robert using a hydrogen-filled balloon. Two hours and 30 minutes later, they landed some 22 miles from Paris. The balloon is shown above in flight. (Photograph courtesy of Edita/Bibliothèque des PTT, Berne.)

It was obvious early on that gas ballooning offered a more dependable and longer lasting source of lifting power than hot air. One of the first challenges was to see how far one could fly. That led to setting the goal of trying to fly across the English Channel. The first successful crossing of the English Channel was achieved in 1785 in a flight piloted by French balloonist Jean-Pierre Blanchard along with an American doctor, John Jeffries. In the artist's depiction above, the balloon is shown flying over the French countryside after crossing the English Channel. After this history-making flight, the efforts for flying focused on gas balloons. (Photograph courtesy of Bibliothèque nationale de France.)

The first manned flight of a balloon in America occurred on January 9, 1793. It was a hydrogen-gas balloon piloted by the same Frenchman who was the first to cross the English Channel, Jean-Pierre Blanchard. This flight ascended from a prison yard in Philadelphia, Pennsylvania. He ascended to about 5,800 feet, and he made a successful landing in Gloucester County, New Jersey. Pres. George Washington observed the launch and also handed a written document to Blanchard calling on American citizens to do all they could to assist his endeavor as opportunity might be accorded them. (Illustration reprinted with permission from the *First Air Voyage in America, January 9, 1793*, Applewood Books, Carlisle, Massachusetts.)

By the 1900s, gas-filled, cigar-shaped airships began to be built, with some of them having a ridged frame to keep their shape. The internal combustion engine had been invented, and it was now possible to put engines and propellers on these large airships as well as rudders, so that their direction and speed could be controlled. It was these airships that become the first commercial airliners. The airship pictured above at the 1904 World's Fair in St. Louis is the California Arrow, piloted by Roy Knabenshue. (Photograph courtesy of the National Balloon Museum Archives.)

By 1936, airships were more common. The largest and most famous of these was the Hindenburg built in Germany. It was 803 feet long, 135 feet wide, and held 7 million cubic feet of gas. In addition, it had luxurious passenger compartments including a lounge with a grand piano, passenger cabins, a promenade deck, a smoking room, and a reading and writing room as well as crew quarters. On May 6, 1937, the Hindenburg caught fire and burned while attempting to dock in Lakehurst, New Jersey. Thirty-five of its 97 passengers died in the accident. The danger of using hydrogen gas eventually caused the demise of the great airships and fixed-wing aircraft became the more practical means of flight. (Photograph courtesy of Archiv der Luftschiffbau Zeppelin GmbH, Friedrichshafen.)

World's Largest Balloon
Leaving Stratosphere Bowl
Rapid City. S. Dak. July 28th 1934
RISE PHOTO

While the airships were carrying passengers, scientists were using teardrop-shaped gas balloons for exploring the stratosphere and gathering scientific data. Famous aeronauts such as Paul Kipfer, Auguste Piccard, Jean and Jeannette Piccard, Maj. William E. Kepner, Albert W. Stevens, Capt. Orvil Anderson, and others were making history with altitude record–setting flights. Above is a picture of the balloon *Explorer I* ascending from the Strato Bowl in South Dakota at 5:45 a.m. on July 28, 1934. It was cosponsored by the National Geographic Society and the U.S. Army Air Corps and was manned by Capt. Albert Stevens, Capt. Orvil Anderson, and Maj. William Kepner. That flight reached an altitude of 60,613 feet, but tears developed in the hydrogen-filled balloon, and they had to descend. At about 3,000 feet, the balloon burst, forcing the men to parachute to earth. The gondola crashed in a cornfield in Nebraska. (Photograph by Rise Photograph Studio; courtesy of the National Balloon Museum Archives.)

Shown above are Capt. Albert Stevens (left with glasses) and Lt. Orvil Anderson (right) with the pressurized gondola they used in the flight of *Explorer I*. Such a pressurized cabin was needed to provide life support at altitudes in the stratosphere. Another record was set by *Explorer II*, which also launched from the Strato Bowl in South Dakota, at 7:01 a.m. on November 11, 1935. That flight used a larger balloon than *Explorer I* and was filled with helium gas. The crew was cut from three to two for this flight, and Albert Stevens and Orvil Anderson were the ones chosen. *Explorer II* reached a record altitude of 72,395 feet, and Stevens and Anderson thus became the first men to ever view and photograph the curvature of the earth. They touched down the same day at 3:14 p.m. near White Lake, South Dakota. (Photograph by Rise Photograph Studio; courtesy of the National Balloon Museum Archives.)

The Strato Bowl was an ideal location to launch high altitude balloons because it was a bowl-shaped area with a flat, grassy bottom surrounded by high, canyon-like walls that sheltered the balloon from the winds while it was being inflated. As a youth, Ed Yost watched the 1934 launch and was forever captivated by ballooning. He would go on to invent the modern hot air balloon and become a key person in bringing ballooning to Indianola, as shown in the next chapter. (Photograph courtesy of the state archives of the South Dakota State Historical Society.)

Three

Ballooning for the Masses

The invention of the modern hot air balloon in 1960 made it possible for the average citizen to own and fly his or her own balloon because the new system was dependable, relatively inexpensive, and easy to launch compared to the complicated gas balloon systems. The new system, with the new nylon fabric and the propane burner system, made it easy to heat the air in a balloon and keep it aloft for a long enough time to be useful. In addition, the new system was easy to launch by a small number of people and was reusable.

The U.S. Navy Office of Naval Research commissioned Ed Yost and Raven Industries in Sioux Falls, South Dakota, to develop a hot air balloon capable of carrying one man and enough fuel to fly for 3 hours, carry a load to an altitude of 10,000 feet, and be reusable. In addition, the system had to have a fast inflation time, launching time, and require only a minimum crew to operate. The photograph above shows one of Yost's early experimental tethered hot air balloon flights in that project in which he used a plastic balloon and plumbers' pots for a heat source. This proved unsatisfactory, so Yost and his fellow crew at Raven worked on revisions, which led to success in 1960. (Photograph courtesy of Ed Yost.)

It should be noted that several people tried to develop a petroleum-based heat source for a hot air balloons between 1783 and 1960; however, none of them were successful. Ed Yost became the first person to accomplish it. In this picture, Ed Yost is shown piloting the first free flight of the new balloon in Bruning, Nebraska, on October 22, 1960. Yost and his team of engineers had developed a new envelope made of nylon and invented a dependable heat source in the form of a propane gas burner. This first balloon was 40 feet in diameter and had a volume of 30,000 cubic feet of air. The gross weight of the balloon, including Yost and fuel, was 404 pounds. The gondola consisted of a pilot's chair with two propane tanks and burner attached. It was not until this invention of the modern hot air balloon by Iowa-born Paul E. "Ed" Yost in 1960 with a practical heat source and balloon envelope that ballooning became possible for the average person. (Copyright © 1960 by Rekwin Archive.)

Ed Yost, shown here in 1964, after inventing the modern hot air balloon system, went on to invent a number of items for ballooning. He held 21 patents on balloons and lighter-than-air mechanisms. He has never asked for any compensation from companies that manufacture devices using his patents. He saw his inventions as solving problems and creating techniques and devices to make ballooning safer and possible. He has received many awards from organizations such as the Balloon Federation of America, the Fédération Aéronautique Internationale, the Wingfoot Lighter-than-Air Society, the National Aeronautic Association, and the Aero Club of New England. In 2003, Yost became the first inductee into the U.S. Ballooning Hall of Fame (see pages 94–95) at the National Balloon Museum in Indianola, Iowa. (Photograph courtesy of Ed Yost.)

Four

Sport Ballooning
Comes of Age
in the 1960s

Just three years after the invention of the modern hot air balloon in 1960 by Ed Yost, he, together with Don Piccard, flew a modern hot air balloon named the *Channel Champ* across the English Channel going from Rye in England to Gravelines in France. It was the first long distance flight by a hot air balloon. The publicity generated by this flight caused worldwide attention to the fact that a dependable, practical, and relatively inexpensive balloon was something almost anyone could own and know the pleasure of flying. Almost immediately, ballooning became a sport. New balloon makers came on the scene, and ballooning events started to spring up where balloonists would get together, fly, and enjoy the new sport. The first National Hot Air Balloon Championship was held in Michigan in 1963; the Whiskey Hill–Atherton–Menlo Oaks Ballooning and Sporting Society (WHAMOBASS) balloon rally started in California in 1964; and the event that was to become the world's largest ballooning event started with 13 balloons in 1972. And there were many others.

After that first flight, hot air ballooning soon became a sport for the masses. Ed Yost and the ballooning team at Raven Industries kept improving the system design. They decided to attempt to cross the English Channel in order to demonstrate the practical nature of the new system. In April 1963, Ed Yost and Don Piccard made the first flight of a hot air balloon across the English Channel from Rye, England, to Gravelines, France, in their balloon the *Channel Champ*. Above, the balloon is being inflated in preparation for flight. (Photograph courtesy of the National Balloon Museum Archives and Orvin Olivier.)

At left are Ed Yost and Don Piccard making final preparations for the flight seated on their gondola, which simply consisted of a curved board with two fuel tanks attached to it. The board is a "stone boat," something that farmers used to pull behind their horses on which they would place stones they wanted to remove from the field. This gondola and the envelope (in its bag) are now on exhibit at the National Balloon Museum. (Photograph courtesy of the National Balloon Museum Archives and Orvin Olivier.)

The *Channel Champ* flight lasted 3 hours and 17 minutes and reached an altitude of 13,500 feet. The balloon was a 60,000-cubic-foot envelope with a diameter of 50 feet. The cubic foot capacity was twice that used in Yost's first flight in 1960. This single flight across the channel brought worldwide attention to the fact that a practical and relatively inexpensive way to float over the landscape in a lighter-than-air craft was available. It was after that that ballooning really started to become popular. (Photograph courtesy of the National Balloon Museum Archives and Orvin Olivier.)

The *Channel Champ* landed in a field without a ground crew. When it touched down, Ed Yost pulled the release that activated the explosive release mechanism, which opened the squib (the gathered top of the balloon) to release the hot air. In the interval between the release and the time it took for the balloon to deflate, the board gondola was drug across the field some distance by the wind until the balloon was no longer capable of catching enough wind to move it. The balloon was draped across a fence and placed in the next field in the direction the wind was blowing. In this picture, Ed Yost is standing by the board gondola on which they were riding. Don Piccard, who jumped off before the gondola had come to a complete stop, is shown at left running with his hands raised in the shape of an "O," the international sign that everything is "okay." (Photograph courtesy of the National Balloon Museum Archives and Ed Yost.)

After landing the *Channel Champ*, Ed Yost and Don Piccard deliver balloon airmail they carried on the flight to a French postman. Ed is on the left and Don is on the right holding the bag of mail as he hands it to the postman. The first hydrogen gas balloon to cross the Channel back in 1785 also carried mail, so this flight continued that tradition. Carrying mail is just one more way of saying that a modern hot air balloon is a practical aircraft. However, due to limited steering abilities and limited air time allowed by the amount of propane fuel one can carry on board, it is not likely balloons will be used to deliver mail on a regular basis. (Photograph courtesy of the National Balloon Museum Archives and Ed Yost.)

By the mid-1960s, there were 3 hot air balloon makers in the United States: Raven (later named Aerostar), Semco, and Piccard, with Tracy Barnes' Balloon Works (now known as Firefly) coming soon after. Clockwise from top left, the hot air balloons pictured were made by Raven, Semco, Balloon Works, and Piccard. (Photographs courtesy of Raven Industries, Inc.; Semco Balloons, Inc.; Balloon Works, Inc.; and Afors Balloon and Rocket Club.)

When a new sport takes the hearts of men and women, it is not long before they begin to gather together to share their sport. The first National Hot Air Balloon Championship was held in 1963 in Kalamazoo, Michigan. The lone balloon above is just one of the balloons flown there. That event was under the auspices of the National Aeronautic Association. That organization formed the Balloon Federation of America (BFA) in 1961 as a federation of gas balloons clubs. It was not until 1967 that the Balloon Federation of American was reorganized into a hot air balloon group. The BFA now also has a gas balloon division. In 1964, the national championship moved to Nevada where it remained through 1966, but no championship was scheduled for the next three years. The Balloon Federation of America organized the next championship event in 1970, which is when Indianola came into the picture. (Photograph courtesy of Ed Yost.)

In 1964, Deke Sonnichsen (shown at left) in California founded the WHAMOBASS rally, which has been held every year since, making it the longest continuously running ballooning event in America, though it has been held in several different locations in California. The name WHAMOBASS comes from all the different locations that have hosted the event over the years until finally settling in Coalinga, California. The name stands for Whiskey Hill–Atherton–Menlo Oaks Ballooning and Sporting Society. Sonnichsen ran the event until 2000. The Pacific Coast Aeronauts are now the governing body that supports and promotes WHAMOBASS, and Sonnichsen is still an active participant. (Above, photograph courtesy of Brian P. Lawler; left, photograph courtesy of Deke Sonnichsen.)

While the U.S. nationals were well under way in Indianola, Sid Cutter, the first person to own a hot air balloon in New Mexico, took part in the first balloon rally in Albuquerque, New Mexico, in 1972. Cutter, shown above, was asked to fly his balloon, *Road Runner*, as part of a 50th birthday celebration for KOB Radio. The event was cosponsored for the radio station by the Albuquerque Aerostat Ascension Association. (Photograph courtesy of the National Balloon Museum Archives.)

This event was advertised as the Albuquerque International Coyote *Road Runner* Balloon Race. The poster above was made for the occasion. This particular poster was signed by the balloon pilots, and the signatures are in the lower portion of the picture. It was decided to invite other balloonists in addition to Cutter. It turned out that 13 balloonists from around the country participated. Sid Cutter, in *Road Runner*, was chased by the other 12 balloons, which were referred to as coyotes. (Photograph courtesy of Tom McConnell.)

Among the pack of coyotes chasing Sid Cutter were Dennis Floden, Bill Cutter, Gene Dennis, Don Kersten, Oscar Kratz, Bill Murtorff, Don Piccard, Wilma Piccard, Karl Stefan, Brent Stockwell, Carter Twedt, and Matt Wiederkehr. The pictures here are two views of this first *Road Runner* Race getting under way. This, the first Albuquerque Roadrunner-Coyote Balloon Race, soon became known as the first balloon fiesta. Don Piccard was the winner. He landed his balloon only 184 feet from the *Road Runner*. Don's wife, Wilma, in her own balloon, placed second by landing 206 feet away. (Photographs courtesy of Dick Brown.)

That *Road Runner* event was the first in what became an annual balloon rally, which eventually evolved into what is now known as the Albuquerque International Balloon Fiesta. The picture above shows balloons inflated during the 1974 fiesta, which took place at the New Mexico State Fairgrounds. The fiesta has grown over the years and is now the largest balloon rally in the world. The largest number of balloons participating was 1,019 in the year 2000. After that they limited registration to 750 balloonists. The fiesta attracts both gas and hot air balloonists from all over the world. (Photograph courtesy of Tom McConnell.)

The launch field for the Albuquerque International Fiesta is immense as seen in this aerial photograph of the event taken in 2004. Balloons fill the sky for about as wide as one's vision can take in at one time. Most of the balloons flown at the fiesta are hot air balloons, but there are some who fly gas balloons as a part of America's Challenge Gas Balloon Race and sometimes the Coupe de Gordon Bennett, which are events held within the fiesta. The America's Challenge Gas Balloon Race, where special long-distance gas balloons are inflated and then launched, is annually flown during the fiesta. The winner of the race is whose balloon travels the farthest. Spectators are allowed on the balloon field as can be seen above. Order is kept by volunteer launch directors called zebras, who wear black-and-white striped clothes to identify themselves. The zebras also work with the scoring officials and the safety team. During the 1960s and 1970s, countless other balloon rallies sprang up all across the country as well. (Photograph by and courtesy of Cindy Petrehn Photography at cphotovail.com.)

This view of the fiesta in 2009 shows balloons floating over the Anderson-Abruzzo-Albuquerque International Balloon Museum, seen in the lower center of this picture. It opened in 2000 and is adjacent to the fiesta balloon field. The museum depicts the development of ballooning through scientific and artistic objects, telling the story of worldwide achievements in ballooning. Included in its exhibits are gondolas from some of the most famous balloon flights the world has seen, representing such names as Jules Verne, Steve Fossett, and others. It also includes the collections of the former Soukup and Thomas International Balloon and Airship Museum from Mitchell, South Dakota. It differs from the National Balloon Museum in Indianola in that it has a more international emphasis, while the National Balloon Museum focuses more on the history of ballooning since the invention of the modern hot air balloon in 1960. However, both museums cover ballooning from the first flight in 1783 to the present. (Photograph by and courtesy of Becky Wigeland.)

Five

SPORT BALLOONING COMES TO INDIANOLA

Sport ballooning came to Indianola with the U.S. National Hot Air Balloon Championships, which came in 1970. Community leaders together with Simpson College welcomed the championship event with open arms that year. The Balloon Federation of America was so impressed with the way the event was put together they decided to come again in 1971, and the annual event remained in Indianola for 18 years, 1970 through 1988. During that time, the steady base of volunteers needed to host such an event was developed, and the event gradually grew from 16 balloonists the first year to 100.

In 1970, only 10 years after the first flight of Yost's modern hot air balloon and after a three-year absence of the U.S. National Hot Air Balloon Championships, they resumed in 1970 at Indianola, Iowa, on the Simpson College campus athletic field under the auspices of the Balloon Federation of America. Several of the balloons at the 1970 U.S. National Hot Air Balloon Championship are shown above inflated and ready for launch. (Photograph courtesy of Frank Pritchard.)

The U.S. National Hot Air Balloon Championship event came to Indianola through the efforts of Don Kersten and Ed Yost. Don Kersten of Fort Dodge, Iowa, was the president of the Balloon Federation of America that year, and he and Ed Yost were searching for a site for the event. Technically the event was being sponsored by the Iowa State Fair, but only one flight on the final day of the event could be at the fairgrounds due to space and schedule limitations by the grandstand. At the local level, Gary Ruble and Jim Madsen from the Indianola Chamber of Commerce became involved in the conversation and planning for the event. Tom Ackerman from Simpson College in Indianola offered the Simpson College athletic field to host the preliminary flights. When it came time to organize the event, Dale Hicks arranged for trucks and crew for the balloonists, Don Koontz of Simpson obtained scorers, and many others became involved as well. Clockwise from top left are Don Kersten, Ed Yost, Gary Ruble, and Tom Ackerman. (Photographs courtesy of the National Balloon Museum Archives.)

There were 11 balloons and 18 balloonists at the 1970 championship. Those in attendance were Dr. William C. Grabb, Frank Pritchard, Wilma Eckmeier, Peter Kreig, William Eckmeier, Robert J. Rechs, Don Kersten, Norton Grim, Richard Stamberg, Dennis Floden, R. Dodds Meddock, David Thiel, Steven Langjahr, Bill Meadows, J. Reber Chambers, Deke Sonnichsen, Matt Wiederkehr, and Robert L. "Bob" Walingunda. In addition to the registered pilots, Bill Meadows of South Carolina and Don Piccard of California were present and assisted in some of the organizational work of the event. All the preliminary events that week took place in Indianola, and the 11 finalists in the ballooning competition took part in the final ascension in front of the grandstand at the Iowa State Fairgrounds in Des Moines. Ed Yost served as clerk of course. (Copyright © 1970 by Rekwin Archive.)

On the final day of the 1970 U.S. National Hot Air Balloon Championship, the balloons were laid out on the ground in front of the grandstand at the state fairgrounds in Des Moines in preparation for inflating and lift off. These few days of ballooning in Indianola and Des Moines marked the first time a group of balloons came together for flying in Iowa. (Photograph by and courtesy of Frank Pritchard.)

Shown above is the scene at the Iowa State Fairgrounds of the final day of the 1970 event. Paul E. "Ed" Yost was chairman of the 1970 event in Indianola. He was called the clerk of course, a position that was renamed later as balloonmeister. He is the man wearing the white, brimmed hat only partially visible in the center of the picture above. It seems fitting that the inventor of the modern hot air balloon, who was born in Bristow, Iowa, should play a major role in ballooning coming to Iowa. The Balloon Federation of America declared the 1970 event hosted in Indianola the "most successful event ever staged in the sport of ballooning." Thus began an odyssey that resulted in Indianola becoming the ballooning capital of Iowa. (Photograph courtesy of the National Balloon Museum Archives and Ed Yost.)

The balloon shown here, known as the *Pepsi Balloon*, flown by Frank Pritchard and Dennis Floden, created a stir with some local farmers in 1970. As they flew over the hog lot of Merrill Dorland, the sound of the burners stampeded his hogs into and over a fence into a bean field. This resulted in the loss of 40 pigs and 1 sow as well as damage to the fence and bean field. The losses, plus labor to round up the animals, resulted in damages of $1,060 plus $300 in damages to two neighbors' properties. The pilots heard from the farmer's attorney for relief. The matter was subsequently amicably settled to the satisfaction of all parties. (Photograph courtesy of Frank Pritchard.)

The success of the 1970 nationals held in Indianola led the BFA to choose Indianola to host the 1971 championship. Above is a view of the balloons preparing to launch from the Simpson College athletic field in 1971. Gary Ruble of Indianola, shown at left from a 1976 *Indianola Record Herald and Tribune* article, chaired a committee of several business persons to make plans for hosting the 1971 event. The hospitality provided by this group and the many other volunteers, together with Simpson College again being willing to provide the site, resulted in Indianola hosting the event for a total of 18 years. (Above, photograph courtesy of the National Balloon Museum Archives; below, photograph courtesy of the *Indianola Record Herald and Tribune*.)

Above, the crew makes final preparations before a launch. The pilot stands in a metal frame gondola open on the sides. Various forms of gondolas have been tried over the years, including metal and fiberglass. Most pilots have settled on wicker baskets because they have more give to them and hence absorb more of the jolt in a hard landing, making landing a little gentler for the pilot and any riders. (Photograph courtesy of the National Balloon Museum Archives.)

This aerial view shows balloons getting ready to launch on the Simpson College campus athletic field in 1972. The three white buildings just in front of the balloons are fraternity buildings, which over the years were used to house many of the balloonists and their crews. The large white building in the background is the Simpson College Blank Center for the Performing Arts. The Blank center is also home of the Des Moines Metro Opera's widely acclaimed summer opera festival, which is held there each year. (Photograph courtesy of Dick Stamberg.)

Another aerial view of the balloon launch area at Simpson College shows the crowds of onlookers gathered all around the field to observe the launch. In this picture, the balloons are laid out ready to be inflated. The location was next to a residential area of the city, and it was not uncommon for people to hear and see hot air balloons floating over their homes in the early morning or early evening hours. Today there are a number of balloon pilots living in the Indianola area, so hardly a week goes by in the warm seasons of the year that Indianola residents do not see one or more balloons floating above. (Photograph courtesy of John Schultz.)

In this view, a balloon has landed in a rural area and near a driveway. The chase crew, with the white pickup and trailer, has parked in the entrance to the driveway, and onlookers have gathered to watch the crew walk the balloon over near the trailer where they will deflate the balloon, pack it back into its bag, and load it on the trailer for transport. (Photograph courtesy of the National Balloon Museum Archives.)

During the 1970s, balloon manufacturers and other vendors, including local church food tents, were set up near the Simpson balloon field. Lynn Johnson, wife of BFA member Ray Johnson, was the first person to set up a tent during the nationals to sell ballooning memorabilia. The concession was called Balloons and Things. Her efforts were the forerunner of the present gift shops at the museum and at the current balloon field. (Photographs by and courtesy of Thom Roberts.)

In this picture taken on the Simpson College athletic field in 1974, spectators get a close-up view as pilots begin to inflate their balloons. Balloon watching is a fun sport for all ages. Each year more and more people came to Indianola to see the colorful extravaganza unfold. The sport of hot air ballooning started only after Ed Yost's invention of the modern hot air balloon in 1960, and so what was happening in Indianola during the 1970s was pretty new to everyone. Even the manufacturers of balloons were still experimenting with new devices and improvements and refinements to their baskets, balloons, burners, and related items needed for flying. Indianola was rapidly become a central location for seeing the development of this new sport as it was taking place. (Photograph by and courtesy of Blair Lawson.)

When the winds were calm over the U.S. National Hot Air Balloon Championship, the skies around Indianola were often filled with balloons. In this picture, there are no less that 47 balloons visible in the air at one time. In those early days of ballooning in Iowa during the 1970s and 1980s, there were few places in the nation where that many balloons could be seen together at once. That is still true in Indianola today with the National Balloon Classic held there each summer, which usually hosts over 100 balloons. (Photograph by and courtesy of Thom Roberts.)

An organization called Indianola Balloons, Inc. (IBI) was established to plan and operate the annual event. Pictured above are some of the members of the events committee of IBI who volunteered to help in planning during the 1970s. Seated, from left to right, are Dale Hagen, Kathy King, Arlan Brown, Sandy Opstad, Craig Ryan, Mike Hollinger, Sharon Richman, and Marlene Wall; (standing) Bob Sandy, Garry Graham, Chuck Laverty, Bev Stockton, Lyn Godbey, Cheryl Graham, Gary King, Dale Hicks, Dee Allen, Melvin Herold, Sherry Allsup, Laurie Jones, Sherry Vander Hamm, and Carmen Hampton. Marlene Wall was employed as the secretary in the offices of the Indianola Chamber of Commerce and IBI, and she became the key leader in organizing the volunteer effort each year. That was a task she performed from 1971 through 1986. Gary Ruble was president of the Indianola Chamber of Commerce in 1971 and 1972 and was executive director from 1973 through 1978, which gave him a major leadership role in planning the annual ballooning event as well. Over the years, since the beginning of hot air ballooning in Indianola, many people have served as president of the organizing group. From 1973 to 1983, the organizing group was Indianola Balloons, Inc. with presidents Roy Godwin, Dick Pratt, Bruce Gause, Jim Weinman, Duane Palmer, Charles Laverty, Dale Hicks, Max Bishop, Gary King, and Arlan Brown. From 1984 to 1988, it was the National Balloon Championship, Ltd., with presidents Alden "Al" Godwin, Don Prine, Jim Thompson, Dennis Shull, and Orrie Koehlmoos. From 1989 to the present, it has been the National Balloon Classic with presidents Larry McConnell, Eldon McElroy, Jim Thorius, Gerald Knoll, Terry Boettcher, Al Luzum, Kevin Ades, Rich Nelson, Mike Rozga, Martha West, Drew Gocken, Esther Snyder, Joe Schnieders, John Parker Jr., Donna Rieck, Darcy Moeller, Dale Crain, and Heather Palmer. (Photograph courtesy of *Indianola Record Herald and Tribune*.)

Six

BALLOONING SPREADS ACROSS IOWA

As gliding on the wind began to be popular among more and more Iowans, it was only natural that local ballooning clubs and events would spring up, and indeed they did. The Hawkeye Aerostation Society in central Iowa was the first in 1972. The second club to form was Balloons Over Iowa. The third was the Iowa Balloonists Association. In addition to the balloon clubs, balloon events also sprang up in cities all over Iowa. These were usually annual events held by balloonists or were held in conjunction with various city celebrations. Iowa holds claim to one balloon maker who began building balloons in the basement of his home in Indianola. His company is known today as National Balloons Limited, which now has a manufactory facility in nearby Patterson, Iowa. Some of the ballooning events have come and gone over the years, but there are a number of those still occurring in Iowa.

The first person in Iowa to own a hot air balloon was Don Kersten, an attorney from Fort Dodge, Iowa. His balloon, which is pictured to the left, was called *Merope*, after his first wife. In July 1965, Kersten bought the balloon from Don Piccard, who brought the balloon to Fort Dodge, Iowa, and taught him how to fly it. After the third flight, Piccard said, "Okay, you've got a commercial license." In September 1965, Kersten competed in the U.S. National Championship in Reno, Nevada, where he took third place. He was a founding father of the Balloon Federation of America and served as its president from 1967 to 1971. In the late 1960s, Kersten was one of about a dozen active hot air balloonists in the United States. As was noted earlier, Kersten played a major role in getting the U.S. National Hot Air Balloon Championship to Indianola in 1970. Kersten also founded the All Iowa Balloon Rally, held for several years in the mid- to late 1970s in Fort Dodge, Iowa. (Left, photograph courtesy of Frank Pritchard; below, photograph courtesy of the Kersten family.)

The first person in Indianola to own a hot air balloon was Pat McClintic (shown above right). Like Don Kersten, she purchased a Piccard balloon. She was another one of the key leaders in the group of people who planned and carried out the hosting of the U.S. National Hot Air Balloon Championship for a number of years. As shown in chapter nine, she will become one of the initial board members for the National Balloon Museum when it is first incorporated. (Photograph from the National Balloon Museum Archives.)

The first balloon club founded in Iowa was the Hawkeye Aerostation Society, Inc., which was formed in 1973 in central Iowa with members from both Polk and Warren counties, three of whom were from Indianola. They started with 10 members, each of whom bought a share in a Raven balloon. Some of the members earned their pilot's licenses and some were just satisfied to be partners and crew for the rest of the partners. The initial members were La Vonne Arendsee, Walter Burgin, Jack Cole, Robert Fleming, Elton Freeman, Phil Gray, Harold Heisey, E. T. Meredith III, Lowell Sanquist, and James Wallace Jr. Phil Gray was the first one to be trained as a pilot, and he then trained the others. Phil would eventually start building balloons, first in his basement at home but now in a manufacturing facility in nearby Patterson, Iowa. Shown in the picture above are seven of the members. Clockwise from the lower left corner are Jack Cole, LaVonne Arendsee, Robert Fleming, Elton Freeman, James Wallace Jr., Phil Gray, and Blair Lawson. (Photograph by and courtesy of Brian Freeman.)

The Hawkeye Aerostation Society's original balloon (shown at right) was a red, white, and black Raven S50A that held 56,400 cubic feet of air, was 50 feet in diameter, and stood 58 feet tall. Total cost for the system—including inflator fan, fuel tanks, taxes, fees, and other equipment—was $6,380. Their first flight occurred on June 16, 1973. In 1976, they traded their balloon in for a purple and white S55 system (shown below) named *Wanderlust*, which cost $7,501 less with trade in. Shortly after the club became active, Mr. Heisey resigned and was replaced by Blair Lawson. Tom Hanks, who at the time was a farmer near Ackworth, Iowa, became a member later, and eventually only Lawson and Hanks remained. Their second balloon was retired in August 1984, and the club ceased operation at that time. (Photographs by and courtesy of Blair Lawson.)

The second balloon club to form in Iowa was Balloons Over Iowa (BOI), which was founded in February 1978. Those pictured above are the founding fathers of the club. From left to right, they are Don Prine, Jerry Riley, Rob Bartholomew, Bill Griffin, and Terry Boettcher. Denny Pash of Cedar Rapids, Iowa, not pictured, joined in 1980. The club differed from Hawkeye Aerostation Society in that BOI members each owned their own balloon. The club has an oath that members take when they join, which is: "We promise to indulge in the sport of the gods." The club is a fun-loving group with a sense of humor, as evidenced by the fact that their president and vice president are both dogs. In 1979, they sponsored the first Ode to Spring balloon bash, which they still do every spring. This group now has approximately 468 members. Balloons Over Iowa is also the name of Rob and Linda Bartholomew's balloon repair station, which they opened in 1978. (Photograph by and courtesy of Connie Boettcher.)

A third balloon club is the Iowa Balloonists Association (IBA). It was founded on June 11, 1979, with Denny Cox as president, Brian Freeman as vice president, and Bill Griffin as secretary, treasurer, and newsletter editor. IBA was formed after several safety seminars at Denny Cox's Shorty's Restaurant in Pleasantville and several meetings at the annual Iowa championship in Fort Dodge hosted by Dave Beukleman. The balloon at right is Denny Cox's balloon. IBA is a nonprofit corporation established for the purpose of providing enjoyment and recreation for its members. Anyone interested in the advancement of ballooning and IBA may join. The group currently has 180 members. The purpose of IBA is to promote, develop, and aid the art and science of ballooning in Iowa; to promulgate specific rules relating to Iowa Balloon competition; and to promote communication between and with Iowa balloonists and aeronautic agencies. (Photograph by and courtesy of Thom Roberts.)

IBA's current board of directors are, from left to right, Janice Shelton, treasurer; Bob Shelton, president; Sheri Moen, secretary; and Kirk Bloom, vice president. (Photograph courtesy of Bob Shelton.)

Over the years, ballooning events were scheduled in a number of Iowa cities. No one has a complete list, and some have come and gone while others still exist. Above, balloons are inflating at the All Iowa Balloon Rally in Fort Dodge in 1979. The year 2010 will mark 41 years of ballooning in Indianola. (Photograph by and courtesy of Thom Roberts.)

U.S. BALLOONING EVENTS

All Iowa Balloon Rally—Fort Dodge
Annual Balloons and Bridges Flight—Winterset
Annual Jill Rubin Memorial Flight—Newton
Annual Ottumwa Professional Balloon Race—Ottumwa
Balloons in June—Clinton
Balloons Over the Mississippi—Fort Madison
Creston Iowa Balloon Festival—Creston
Great Missouri River Raft Regatta—Sioux City
My Waterloo Days—Waterloo
National Balloon Classic—Indianola
Ode to Spring Balloon Rally—annual event of the Balloons Over Iowa Club
the Great Iowa Balloon Race—Storm Lake
U.S. National Hot Air Balloon Championships—1970–1988
Wild Rose Casino Invitational Balloon Race—Emmetsburg.

OTHER EVENTS WERE HELD IN THE FOLLOWING CITIES:

Altoon	Burlington	Grinnell	Mason City
Amana	Council Bluffs	Ida Grove	Newton
Ames	Davenport	Iowa Falls	Perry
Bagley	Dubuque	Marshalltown	Persia

66

Space does not permit including pictures from all the ballooning events in Iowa, nor would it be easy to gather a complete collection of such pictures. Pictured here are just a few of the Iowa ballooning events. The above photograph is at Muscatine, on the banks of the Mississippi River, in 1982. The photograph at right is at Ottumwa in 1979. (Photographs by and courtesy of Thom Roberts.)

Phil Gray of Indianola, one of the founding members of the Hawkeye Aerostation Society, began building balloons in the basement of his house in 1986. His company is National Balloons Limited, which now has a factory in nearby Patterson, Iowa. The above picture shows Gary Pierce (left) and John Bonk, representatives of the Federal Aviation Administration, presenting Phil and his wife, Linda, their type AC33E certification to build balloons. Prior to that time, they were certified only to build experimental balloon systems. Below, Phil is shown weaving a basket. There are three balloon repair stations within a 20-mile radius of Indianola: Phil and Linda Gray's National Balloons Limited in Patterson; Rob and Linda Bartholomew's Balloons Over Iowa in Carlisle; and Bill and Louise Clemons' Midwest Balloon Services in Patterson. (Above, photograph by and courtesy of Thom Roberts; below, photograph by and courtesy of Becky Wigeland.)

Seven

BALLOONING IN
INDIANOLA EVOLVES

The long-standing connection of the U.S. National Hot Air Balloon Championships being in Indianola led the Balloon Federation of America to establish its national office in Indianola in 1984. After being in Indianola for 18 years, the Balloon Federation of America decided it would be fair to move the event around to various parts of the country to better serve its national constituency. However, the national offices of the BFA continue to be in Indianola. The local leadership in Indianola, which coordinated the large volunteer organization that operated the nationals for the BFA was known as Indianola Balloons, Inc. That group decided to continue the tradition of an annual balloon event in the city, so in 1989, this group initiated the National Balloon Classic, which has been held ever since.

The Balloon Federation of America established its national office in Indianola in 1984 at 112 East Salem Street, where it remained until 2004 when it moved into the National Balloon Museum. Sharon Ripperger (above right) has been the office manager from 1984 to the present. (Photographs by and courtesy of Becky Wigeland.)

The BFA is governed by a 12-member board of directors, 10 of whom are shown above at the National Balloon Museum in spring 2009. From left to right are (first row) Shelley Caraway, Nancy Griffin, Jim Thompson, Don Edwards, and Gary Eaton; (second row) Ken Walter, Andy Baird, Troy Bradley, Gary Ruble, and Bill Hughes. Since the picture was taken, the board had new elections and the current membership is Ken Walter, Donald L. Edwards, Matt Fenster, Shelley Caraway, Bill Hughes, Cory Miller, Troy Bradley, Kevin Knapp, Andy Baird, James A. "Jim" Thompson, Bert Padelt, and Paul Petrehn. (Photograph by and courtesy of Dennis D. Nicholson.)

After being in Indianola for 18 years, the Balloon Federation of America decided it would be more fair to move the event around to various parts of the country to better serve its national constituency. Since moving, the championships have been held in the following cities (the number indicates how many years in each): Baton Rouge, Louisiana (3); Middletown, Ohio (3); Columbia, Missouri (3); Rantaul, Illinois (2); Anderson, South Carolina (6), Waco, Texas (1); again in Anderson, South Carolina (1); and Battle Creek, Michigan (1). The national BFA office remains in Indianola. Pilot Bruce Comstock from Ann Arbor, Michigan, shown at right, was the winner of the U.S. National Hot Air Balloon Championship the most times from 1963 through 1988. He was the winner in 1972, 1976, 1977, 1979, 1982, and 1987. At the last national championship held in Indianola in 1988, Rob Bartholomew of Carlisle, Iowa, shown below, was the winner. He was the first Iowan to win. (Photographs courtesy of the National Balloon Museum Archives.)

Schedule of Events
(Subject to Change)

FRIDAY, August 4
6:00 p.m.   Hardee's Press Night Flight (Invitational Media Flight)
6:00 p.m.   Special Shaped Balloons
6:30 p.m.   Carnival Rides
to 9:00 p.m.   and Amusements
8:00 p.m.   "Nite-Glo" Extravaganza

SATURDAY, August 5
US WEST COMMUNICATIONS
6:00 a.m.   Pleasure Flying/Special Shaped Balloons
8:00 a.m.   Carnival Rides
to 9:00 p.m.   and Amusements
9:00 a.m.   Arts and Crafts Show
to 6:00 p.m.   (Buxton Park)
11:00 a.m.   Town Picnic
to 2:00 p.m.   (Buxton Park)
3:00 p.m.   Model Airplane Exhibition
3:00 p.m.   Balloon Demonstrations
5:00 p.m.   Airplane Stunt Show
5:30 p.m.   Air National Guard Fly-By
6:00 p.m.   Opening Ceremonies/Sky Divers
6:00 p.m.   Hare/Hound Event/Special Shaped Balloons
7:00 p.m.   Farmers Appreciation Night
to 11:00 p.m.   (co-sponsored by Garst Seed Co.)
8:30 p.m.   "Nite-Glo" Extravaganza

SUNDAY, August 6
LENTZ CHEVROLET DAY
6:00 a.m.   Competition Flights/Special Shaped Balloons
7:30 a.m.   Peoples Bank 10K Volkswalk
8:00 a.m.   Carnival Rides
to 9:00 p.m.   and Amusements
9:00 a.m.   Arts and Crafts Show
to 6:00 p.m.   (Buxton Park)
12:00 noon   KJJC (FM106.9) McCoy True Value Country Showdown
2:00 p.m.   Brenton Bank Balloon Parade
3:00 p.m.   Balloon Demonstration
5:00 p.m.   Airplane Stunt Show
5:30 p.m.   Sky Divers
6:00 p.m.   TKO Event/Key Grab/$5,000 Cash Grab/Special Shaped Balloons
8:30 p.m.   "Nite-Glo" Extravaganza

MONDAY, August 7
HERITAGE CABLEVISION DAY
6:00 a.m.   Competition Flights/Special Shaped Balloons
8:00 a.m.   Carnival Rides
to 9:00 p.m.   and Amusements
6:00 p.m.   Mass Ascension and/or Fly-In/Special Shaped Balloons
8:30 p.m.   "Nite-Glo" Extravaganza

TUESDAY, August 8
SUN COUNTRY DAY
6:00 a.m.   Competition Flights
8:00 a.m.   Carnival Rides
to 9:00 p.m.   and Amusements
6:00 p.m.   Mass Ascension and/or Fly-In
8:30 p.m.   "Nite-Glo" Extravaganza

WEDNESDAY, August 9
HARDEE'S DAY
6:00 a.m.   Competition Flights
8:00 a.m.   Carnival Rides
to 9:00 p.m.   and Amusements
6:00 p.m.   Key Grab (Dave Ostrem Imports) and $5000 Cash Grab
8:30 p.m.   "Nite-Glo" Extravaganza
8:30 p.m.   Salon Panache Swim Suit Show/Mr. Iowa
9:00 p.m.   DJ and Dance
to midnight

THURSDAY, August 10
6:00 a.m.   Competition Flights
6:00 p.m.   Mass Ascension and/or Fly-In
8:00 p.m.   "Nite-Glo" Extravaganza

FRIDAY, August 11
SPONSORS DAY
6:00 a.m.   Competition Flights/Special Shaped Balloons
6:00 p.m.   Mass Ascension and/or Fly-In/Special Shaped Balloons (Concessionaires Night)
8:30 p.m.   "Nite-Glo" Extravaganza
8:30 p.m.   Sponsors Party (sponsored by
to 11:00 p.m.   Marriott Food Service Corporation

SATURDAY, August 12
AAA IOWA DAY
6:00 a.m.   Brenton Bank
to 10:00 a.m.   Pancake Breakfast
6:00 a.m.   Mass Ascension/Special Shaped Balloons
9:00 a.m.   Folk Art Show
to 6:00 p.m.   (Buxton Park)
12:00 noon   Classic Car Show
to 5:00 p.m.
6:00 p.m.   Mass Ascension and/or Fly-In/Special Shaped Balloons
8:30 p.m.   "Nite-Glo" Extravaganza

SUNDAY, August 13
6:00 a.m.   Mass Ascension/Special Shaped Balloons

4   8:30 a.m. to 4:30 p.m.   NATIONAL BALLOON MUSEUM HOURS (August 4-13, 1989)

When the National Balloon Championships moved away in 1988, the local organizers, known as Indianola Balloons, Inc. decided to continue having a ballooning event in the city and operate it under the name of National Balloon Classic. Shown above is the schedule page, which is typical for the event each year, from the program book printed for the first National Balloon Classic, held in 1989. The classic has continued the tradition ever since, and it also serves as the North Central Regional Championship for the BFA, which allows the leading scorers here to qualify to advance to the U.S. National Hot Air Balloon Championship. This has given Indianola the distinction of being the city with a continuous annual ballooning event longer than any other city in the United States. The WHAMOBASS balloon rally in California has operated longer, but it has moved around to several locations for its event. (Photograph courtesy of the National Balloon Museum Archives.)

72

Eight

INDIANOLA BECOMES SITE OF THE NATIONAL BALLOON MUSEUM

Beginning in 1972, just two years after the first U.S. National Hot Air Ballooning event came to the city, it was decided to display items about ballooning during the nationals. The first displays were in a storage room in the building occupied by the Indianola Chamber of Commerce. The growing collections of memorabilia were housed in a total of seven temporary locations in the city until the dream of a museum building was realized in 1988. This chapter is the story of how the National Balloon Museum dream became a reality and how it has developed up to the present time. The Balloon Federation of America was the parenting organization that founded the museum, and it is the official archives for the federation and where the federation now has its national offices. However, the museum is operated by its own board of directors. It is a separate, nonprofit corporation with 501(c)(3) status and is operated entirely by a volunteer staff. Its operating budget is funded by donations, memberships, gift shop sales, grants, and office rental fees from the National Balloon Classic and the Balloon Federation of America.

By 1972, just two years after the U.S. National Hot Air Balloon Championships came to Indianola, it was decided to display items about ballooning during the annual event. In the years 1972 through 1974, the Indianola Chamber of Commerce cleaned out a storage room it had in the Berry building on the southwest corner of the Indianola Square and used it to set up a display of available balloon memorabilia. The items were put on display during nationals and then were packed up and stored until the next year because no permanent display space was available. Each year a window had to be removed in order to get a gondola into the display area because it was too big for the door. (Photograph by and courtesy of Dennis D. Nicholson.)

In spring 1973, Balloon Federation of America president Dr. Bill Grabb announced plans to establish a balloon museum in Indianola. An expanded version of this image is shown on page 104. (Photograph courtesy of the National Balloon Museum Archives.)

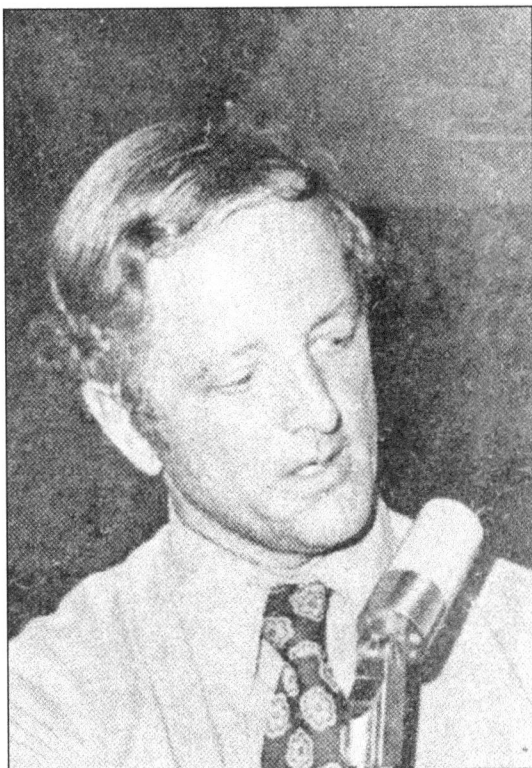

In November 1973, Gary Ruble, then executive director of the Indianola Chamber of Commerce, recommended that a committee be formed to obtain facilities for a National Balloon Museum by March 1974. Those named were Roy Godwin, Jim Ford, and C. D. Myers. They were unable to find a location, so the museum displays remained in the Berry building until 1975. Other leaders in the effort to establish the museum were Pat McClintic (see picture on page 61) of Indianola, chair of the Balloon Museum Committee for Indianola Balloons, Inc. (IBI), and Mary Lou Sargent of Indianola, who helped prepare the annual exhibits. Jerry Kincaide was chairperson of the Balloon Federation of America National Balloon Museum committee along with Dodds Meddock of North Carolina and Don Kersten of Fort Dodge, Iowa. Meddock was named curator and was asked to begin collecting items for the museum. (Photograph courtesy of the National Balloon Museum Archives.)

It is not possible to list all the persons who in some way played a role in the development of the museum. The Balloon Federation of America, Indianola Balloons, Inc. and its subsidiary organization, the National Balloon Classic, have all played important roles in the efforts to establish the Museum. Jim Weinman and his wife, Maxine, of Indianola became two key leaders in the effort. Jim's involvement began in 1975, at which time he worked on plans for a balloon museum with the BFA. In 1976, he was president of Indianola Balloons, Inc. In 1977, he was named chair of the museum committee. Maxine Weinman began assisting Jim with the museum work in 1978. She was named cochair of the committee and eventually became the curator and gift shop manager until she retired in 2003. By 1980, Jim was a member of the museum board of directors, where he served until 2003, and was board president for a number of years. (Photographs courtesy of the National Balloon Museum Archives.)

During the 1975 and 1976 U.S. National Hot Air Balloon Championships, the National Balloon Museum display was opened in the old Rock Island depot building. This was the first official display, as the museum had just been incorporated and established as a legal entity. This location was made possible by Charles Laverty of Indianola, who was the owner of the depot at that time and one of the key leaders in raising and donating funds to eventually build a new museum building. (Photograph courtesy of the Warren County Historical Society.)

In 1977, museum displays were set up just across the street from the balloon field in the lower level of Hopper Gym on the Simpson College campus during the U.S. National Hot Air Balloon Championship. (Above, photograph by and courtesy of Dennis D. Nicholson; below, photograph courtesy of the National Balloon Museum Archives.)

On July 28, 1977, the National Balloon Museum was officially incorporated and an initial 10-person board of directors formed with 5 members representing Indianola Balloons, Inc. and 5 representing the Balloon Federation of America.

THE FIRST MUSEUM BOARD

INDIANOLA BALLOONS, INC.	BALLOON FEDERATION OF AMERICA
Bryce Gause Indianola, Iowa	Dodds Meddock Statesville, North Carolina
Pat McClintic Indianola, Iowa	Peter Stamats Cedar Rapids, Iowa
Dick Pratt Indianola, Iowa	Stephen Langjahr Quartz Hill, California
Gary Ruble Indianola, Iowa	Don Kersten Fort Dodge, Iowa

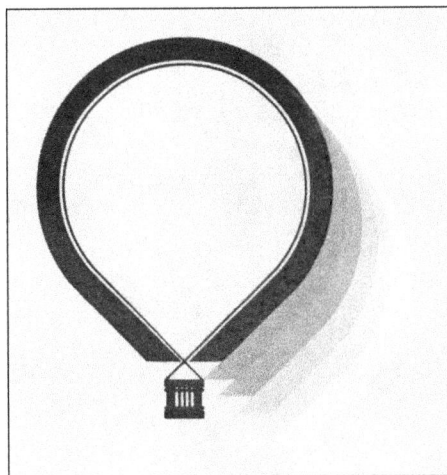

museum logo

On May 27, 1978, the newly formed National Balloon Museum Board of Directors elected the following officers: Peter Stamats, president; Bruce Gause, vice president; Pat McClintic, secretary; and Gary Ruble, treasurer. Eugene T. "Gene" Smith soon joined the Museum board and became the treasurer, a position he held until 1992. He also compiled a history of the Museum. (Photograph courtesy of the National Balloon Museum Archives.)

The museum displays were housed in the lobby of the Blank Theater for the Performing Arts on the Simpson College campus (which is shown above) during the 1978 championships. (Photograph by and courtesy of Dennis D. Nicholson.)

During the 1979 national championships, the museum displays were set up in the former Lentz Chevrolet building at 108 North Jefferson Street, where the Mercy Indianola Medical Clinic is now located. No photograph of this building is available, but above is a portion of the exhibit area in the Lentz building. (Photograph courtesy of the National Balloon Museum Archives.)

Beginning in October 1979, the museum had its first year-round home in a Simpson College house at 711 North E Street (above). The office of Indianola Balloons, Inc. was also located in that house. Below are, from left to right, Marlene Wall, Mary Conklin, and Maxine Weinman. Marlene Wall headed up that office. She coordinated much of the planning for the annual ballooning event. The museum collections remained here until 1984. Mary Conklin worked for the museum and also worked closely with Maxine Weinman beginning in 1979. Mary became the Museum's only paid staff person until March 31, 1989, when funding for the position ended. Since that time, Mary has been a devoted volunteer, logging many hours annually, and is still working several shifts in the Museum each week. (Above, photograph courtesy of the National Balloon Museum Archives; below left, photograph courtesy of Marlene Wall; below center, photograph by and courtesy of Dennis D. Nicholson; below right, photograph courtesy of the National Balloon Museum Archives.)

In March 1983, museum board president Peter Stamats (left) announced plans to hire James R. Ernhart of Ernhart and Associates of Elk River, Minnesota, to conduct a fund-raising feasibility study. The purpose of that was to develop a list of possible donors and set up leadership teams to begin to raise money. (Photograph by and courtesy of Thom Roberts.)

On August 5, 1983, it was announced that Leo and Jill Eisenberg (left) of Kansas City, Missouri, had made a gift of $100,000 for the new museum. Their gift really started the ball rolling for the remainder of the fund-raising effort. Balloonists themselves, the Eisenbergs flew the balloon named the *World's Largest Gumball Machine* (above right). This balloon is now on exhibit in the National Balloon Museum. (Photographs courtesy of the National Balloon Museum Archives.)

Other large donations were given by the following: the City of Indianola gave $100,000 and $65,000 to develop the site; the First Central Bank of Chariton, Iowa, gave the land, valued at $65,000; the Laverty Foundation, established by Charles and Irene Laverty (above) of Indianola, gave $50,000; and the State Historical Society of Iowa gave $50,000. Smaller donations were given by hundreds of individuals, balloon clubs, and other organizations, all of which are listed in a special book on display in the museum. (Photographs courtesy of the Laverty family.)

While the fund-raising efforts were under way in 1984, the museum was moved to this house owned by Simpson College at 711 North C Street. It remained there until the new building opened in 1988. Maxine Weinman, as curator, was responsible for the museum collections during this time, and Mary Conklin was her very able assistant. (Photograph courtesy of the National Balloon Museum Archives.)

Also in 1984, a coordinating committee for the National Balloon Museum was established that included the following persons: Sid Cutter of Albuquerque, New Mexico–chairman (above); Leo Eisenberg of Kansas City, Missouri; Charles O. Laverty of Indianola, Iowa; Don Kersten of Fort Dodge, Iowa; and Pete Stamats of Cedar Rapids, Iowa. An Indianola Leadership Committee was also named for the building program. It included the following: Norma Harmison, cochairman; Dennis Shull, cochairman; Max Bishop; Jim Weinman; Richard Davitt; and Burl Woodyard. A National Endorsement Committee was named that was made up of 53 persons from various parts of the United States as far away as Maryland, Connecticut, California, Texas, Arizona, North Carolina, Georgia, and other points in between. Most notable among the members of the committee was Ed Yost of South Dakota, who, as was noted earlier is "the father of the modern hot air balloon." The purpose of the National Endorsement Committee was to show potential donors that there was a broad base of support for building the museum. (Photograph courtesy of Sid Cutter.)

Ground was broken on August 2, 1986, for the new museum building at the present location on the north edge of Indianola, Iowa. Shown with shovels in the above picture are, from left to right, board members Charles Laverty, Peter Stamats, Leo Eisenberg, Sid Cutter, Don Kersten, architect T. Healey, Indianola mayor Irene Richardson, and Iowa governor Terry Branstad. The picture below shows the large crowd gathered for the ground-breaking ceremonies. (Photographs courtesy of the National Balloon Museum Archives.)

The building of the new museum began in 1986. As construction was under way, the unique form of the building became visible. It was designed to suggest two inverted balloons with baskets. These two tall portions of the building house two large exhibit areas. The entrance arches in front of the building (seen on the right side of the photographs) are designed to give the feeling of entering an inflated balloon lying on its side. The structure is trimmed in blue and yellow ceramic tile that represents the serenity and gracefulness associated with ballooning. Architect T. Healey won an award for his creative use of tiles on the exterior of the building. (Photograph courtesy of the National Balloon Museum Archives.)

This was the scene on moving day in spring of 1988 as artifacts and furnishings were being put into the building for the first time. (Photograph courtesy of Bonnie Love.)

On April 23, 1988, the new museum was opened to the public. The total cost of the building was more than $780,000. It is located on the north edge of Indianola, 12 miles south of Des Moines, Iowa, at 1601 North Jefferson Way (U.S. Highway 65/69). (Photograph courtesy of the National Balloon Museum Archives.)

The grand opening took place on July 19, 1988. The city of Indianola was now home to the National Balloon Museum, a unique facility for the nation destined to put the city on the map so far as ballooning in America was concerned. The museum draws visitors from all 50 states and many foreign countries. Shown above is Leo Eisenberg of Kansas City, the balloonist who made the first large donation to the building. He was given the honor of cutting the ribbon at the grand opening. (Photograph courtesy of the National Balloon Museum Archives.)

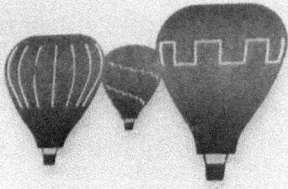

On October 11, 1988, the National Balloon Museum Auxiliary was organized to create an organized system of volunteers to operate the museum. Jean Beatty organized the auxiliary. Each volunteer signs up for one or more shifts each month, ranging from 1 to approximately 12 shifts per month. Each shift is a morning or afternoon of approximately three to three and a half hours each. Pictured on this page are just some of the auxiliary members who work today. In the first row are, from left to right, Linda Nicholson, Mary Lou Staubus, Marylin Gorham, and Roberta Kerr; (second row) Becky Wigeland, Bev Koehlmoos, Joann Sayre, Mary Conklin, and Debra Virkus; (third row) Dennis Nicholson, Charles Kerr, Mike Polson, Blair Lawson, Marilyn Lawson, Carol Polson, Bev Wilson, Mark Weeks, and Dixie Ruble. Those who could not be present for the picture are Laurel Cogswell, Carolyn Fellows, Jo Fisher, Jane Hoffa, Deloris Huse, Pat Kelley, Ruth and Everett Laning, Barb Moody, Sarah Morgan, Joe and Betty Narigon, Susan Olson, Brenda Rohr, Kelly Shaw, Jim Summitt, and Marvin and Barb Van Sickle. (Photograph by and courtesy of Gary Ruble.)

Dennis Anderson

Christine Bertsch

Dan Bertsch

Dick Drake

Denis Frischmeyer
President

Nancy Griffin

Pat Kelley
Gift Shop Manager

Dennis Nicholson

Kelly Shaw

Gary Ruble
Vice President

Bob Shelton

Marlene Wall

Dave Wesner

Mary Conklin
Secretary

Liljana Hidri
Treasurer

Bev Koehlmoos
Auxiliary Rep

Ken Walter
BFA Representative

Becky Wigeland
Curator

NATIONAL BALLOON MUSUEUM BOARD OF DIRECTORS 2009

The National Balloon Museum is a private, nonprofit 501(c)(3) organization run by a board of directors made up of 14 members plus ex-officio members. The board includes balloonists as well as other persons with an interest in the purposes of the museum. Currently the curator, treasurer, secretary, auxiliary representative, and the Balloon Federation of America representative are ex-officio members without votes. Those members of the National Balloon Museum Board of Directors for 2009–2010 (pictured above) follow a long line of persons who have given their time for the good of the museum and carry on the tradition of service begun in 1973. Read more about the museum on the Web at www.nationalballoonmuseum.com. (Photographs courtesy of the National Balloon Museum Archives.)

An endowment fund was created for the museum on April 4, 1992, for the purpose of providing financial support for the special needs of the museum. It was organized by Everett Brown, John Hartung, Gib McConnell, Neal Sinclair, and Gene Smith. The initial goal of $100,000 was established. They immediately raised $10,000 each from Charles Laverty, Orville Crowley, and Bob Downing. Eugene T. Smith was named chairman of the endowment board, and he remained chairman until 2007. The foundation is always looking for additional gifts to increase its investments. Pictured above are five of the current members of the endowment board. From left to right are (seated) Joe Weinman, Eugene Smith, and Mark Weeks; (standing) Gary Ruble and Mary Conklin. Not present for the photograph were Everett Laning, John Hartung, Neal Sinclair, Liljana Hidri, Keith Svare, and Denis Frischmeyer. (Photograph by and courtesy of Dennis D. Nicholson.)

A new, 4,400-square-foot addition was completed in 2003 at a cost of $350,000. The addition is the portion of the building left of the large pine tree in the picture. The new space doubled the size of the museum and included a basement storage area. A grand opening for the addition was held on July 27, 2003. This effort was spearheaded by a museum fund-raising committee headed by Bob Downing of Indianola and included the following persons: Gary Ruble, John Hartung, Doug Shull, Orrie Koehlmoos, Max Morrison, Paul Gorham, Ev Laning, Neal Sinclair, Mary Conklin, Gene Smith, Bob Lester, Nick Nichols, Becky Wigeland, Jennell Connell, Donna Rieck, Mark Weeks, Betty Crawford, Jill Rubin, and Amy Duncan. The fund-raising drive was started with a challenge grant of $50,000 from the Laverty family. A Historical Site Preservation Matching Grant of $100,000 came from the State Historical Society of Iowa. Additional money came from Vision Iowa, Jim and Maxine Weinman, the City of Indianola, Prairie Meadows, and Laverty Estates along with many other contributors. (Photograph by and courtesy of Dennis D. Nicholson.)

At the grand opening for the new addition on July 27, 2003, curator Maxine Weinman was recognized for her 25 years of service and Jim Weinman for his 28 years of service. Their dedication made a significance difference in building the success of ballooning events in the city and to the establishment and the operation of the National Balloon Museum. (Photograph by and courtesy of Becky Wigeland.)

Becky Wigeland (left) was introduced as the new museum curator, succeeding Maxine (right). Becky's first husband, Jerry Riley, was a charter member of Balloons Over Iowa, an Iowa balloon club established in 1978. Just prior to becoming curator, she completed 12 years as president of the museum's board of directors and was newly retired from teaching school. She now devotes much of her time to the volunteer position of museum curator. (Photograph courtesy of the National Balloon Museum Archives.)

Since the new addition opened in 2003, the museum has continued to expand its collections and programs. Several new features and programs have been added or enhanced. Those include the following: U.S. Ballooning Hall of Fame, a theater for interpretive shows, rotating ballooning photograph exhibits, annual Fashion Flare and Brunch, a children's learning center, an expanded exhibit on Women in Ballooning, an expanded ballooning library, and new and revolving exhibits. These new programs and features serve to enhance the role of Indianola as the center of ballooning and ballooning-related activities. Becky Wigeland, as curator, plans exhibits and serves as a primary contact with balloonists and the public. Dennis Nicholson, as assistant to the curator, does much of the graphic and computer work for exhibits and various administrative tasks of the museum operations and develops visual programs for the museum theater. (Photograph by and courtesy of Beverley Wilson.)

The U.S. Ballooning Hall of Fame was established at the museum in 2004 through the sponsorship of the Balloon Federation of America. It was only natural that Ed Yost be the first person to be inducted into the U.S. Ballooning Hall of Fame that year, as he was the man who invented the modern hot air balloon and flew it for the first time. Orvin Olivier of Sioux Falls, South Dakota, representing the Balloon Federation board of directors, inducted him into the Ballooning Hall of Fame. (Photographs by and courtesy of Dennis D. Nicholson)

NATIONAL BALLOON MUSEUM

Paul E. (Ed) Yost
FATHER OF MODERN HOT AIR BALLOONING
BALLOONING HALL OF FAME INDUCTEE
- 2004 -

Above, Ed Yost is pictured after being inducted into the U.S. Ballooning Hall of Fame. Shown with him are three members of the Balloon Federation of America Board of Directors. From left to right are Orvin Olivier, James "Jim" Thompson, Ed Yost, and Nancy Griffin. Since the establishment of the Ballooning Hall of Fame, 15 pioneer balloonists have been inducted. (Photograph courtesy of the National Balloon Museum Archives.)

U.S. Ballooning Hall of Fame Inductees

2004	Paul E. "Ed" Yost	2008	Tracy Barnes
2005	Sidney D. "Sid" Cutter	2009	James W. "Jim" Winker
2005	Don N. Kersten	2009	Karl H. Stefan
2006	Peter Pellegrino	2009	Lucy Luck Stefan
2006	Bruce Comstock	2010	Joseph W. "Joe" Kittinger
2007	Malcolm S. Forbes	2010	Thomas Sheppard
2007	Deke Sonnichsen	2010	Anthony "Tony" Fairbanks
2008	Capt. Eddie Allen		

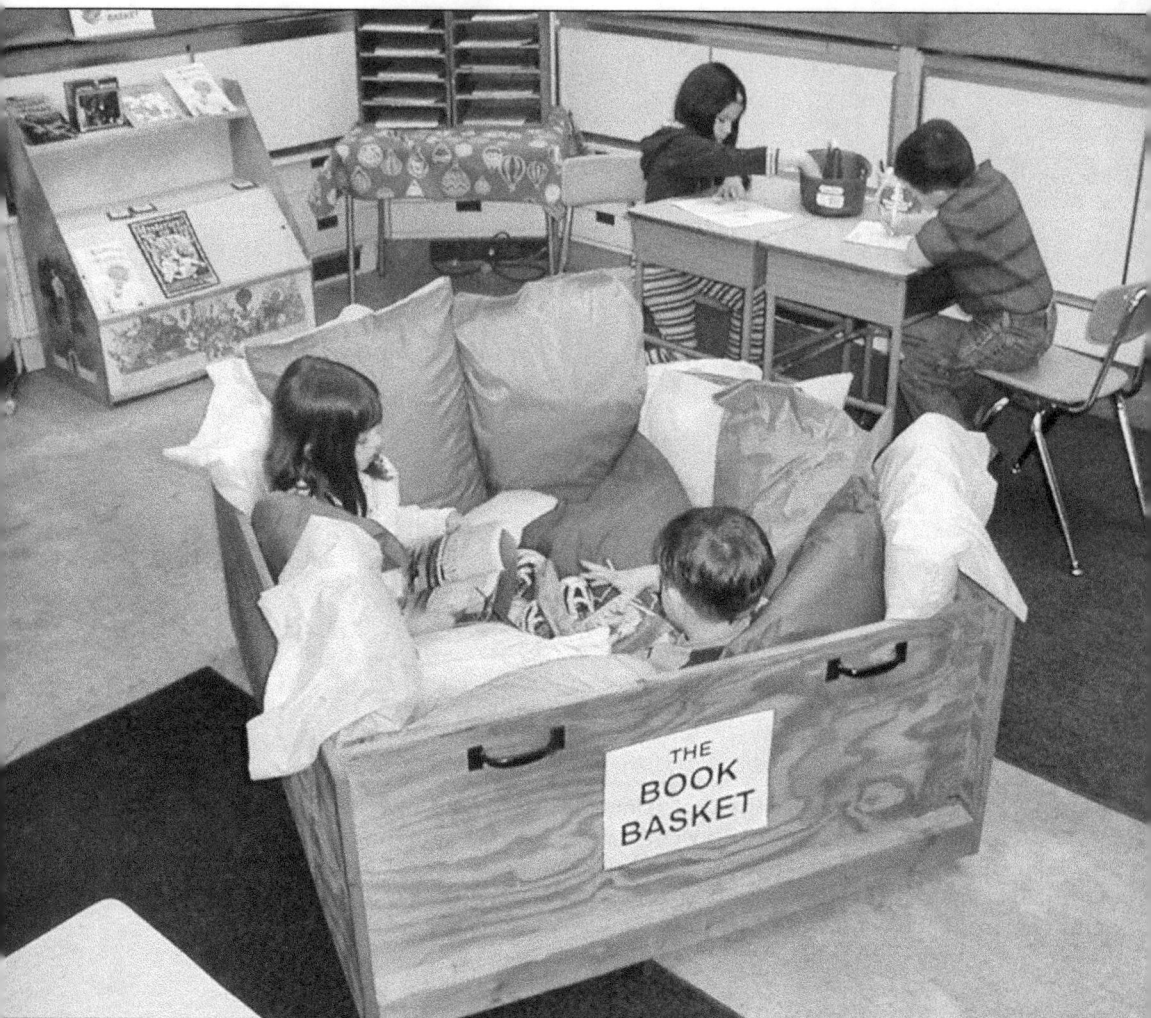

The children's learning center was established to provide an opportunity for children from preschool through the upper elementary years to have a fun way of learning about ballooning. There is a book basket filled with pillows covered with balloon fabric where children can climb in, sit, and read a book about ballooning. There are school desks and tables where they can color balloon pictures with crayons or markers. (Photograph by and courtesy of Dennis D. Nicholson.)

In the children's learning center, there is also a television where children can watch videos about ballooning and a computer where they can play a video game called Hot Air Pilot. The video game lets the player have a virtual experience of flying a hot air balloon in any of four different events. The game gives the player the actual feel of how to manipulate the balloon by operating the burner in order to change altitude as a real balloon pilot would do. (Photograph by and courtesy of Dennis D. Nicholson)

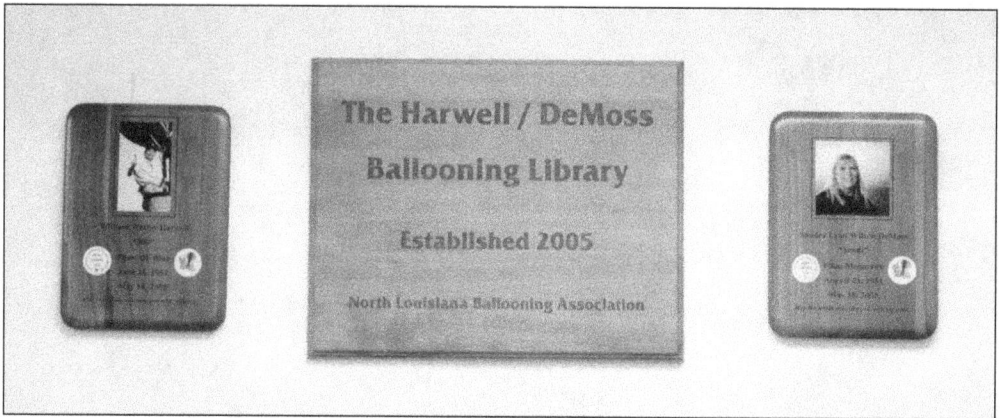

The museum's library was named the Harwell/DeMoss Ballooning Library through a gift of the North Louisiana Ballooning Association in memory of William Wesley Harwell and Sandra Lynn Wilson DeMoss, balloonists who were killed in a ballooning accident on May 18, 2005. The library has been expanded through gifts and purchases in recent years. The collection was expanded greatly in 2009 when the museum received the complete ballooning library of Stephan and Sandy Peck of Battle Creek, Michigan. The library now contains approximately 1,500 books plus many ballooning magazines and other publications about ballooning. (Photograph by and courtesy of Dennis D. Nicholson.)

Above, Bev Wilson, one of the key workers in organizing the library, pauses in front of the library shelves. (Photograph by and courtesy of Dennis D. Nicholson.)

New shelves, to handle the expanded collection, were built by local volunteers Everett Laning and Richard Davitt. Joe Narigon and Becky Wigeland did the finishing work. Funds for the materials for the project were donated by the following balloon clubs and individuals: Iowa Balloonist Association, Balloons Over Iowa Club, Nebraska Balloon Club, Jim and Rita Fromm, Gary Eaton, Reinhart Family, Gary and Dixie Ruble, Cheryl Ganz, Sam Beazley, and one anonymous donor. The library is available to the public for reading and for research. Even though the library is primarily about ballooning, there are also a number of volumes about aviation in general. Some of the books are rare and reserved for use in the library. The library also doubles as a conference room and is used by the museum board of directors, the museum auxiliary board, and the National Balloon Classic, which also has its offices in the museum. The room is also used for receptions for special events. (Photograph by and courtesy of Dennis D. Nicholson.)

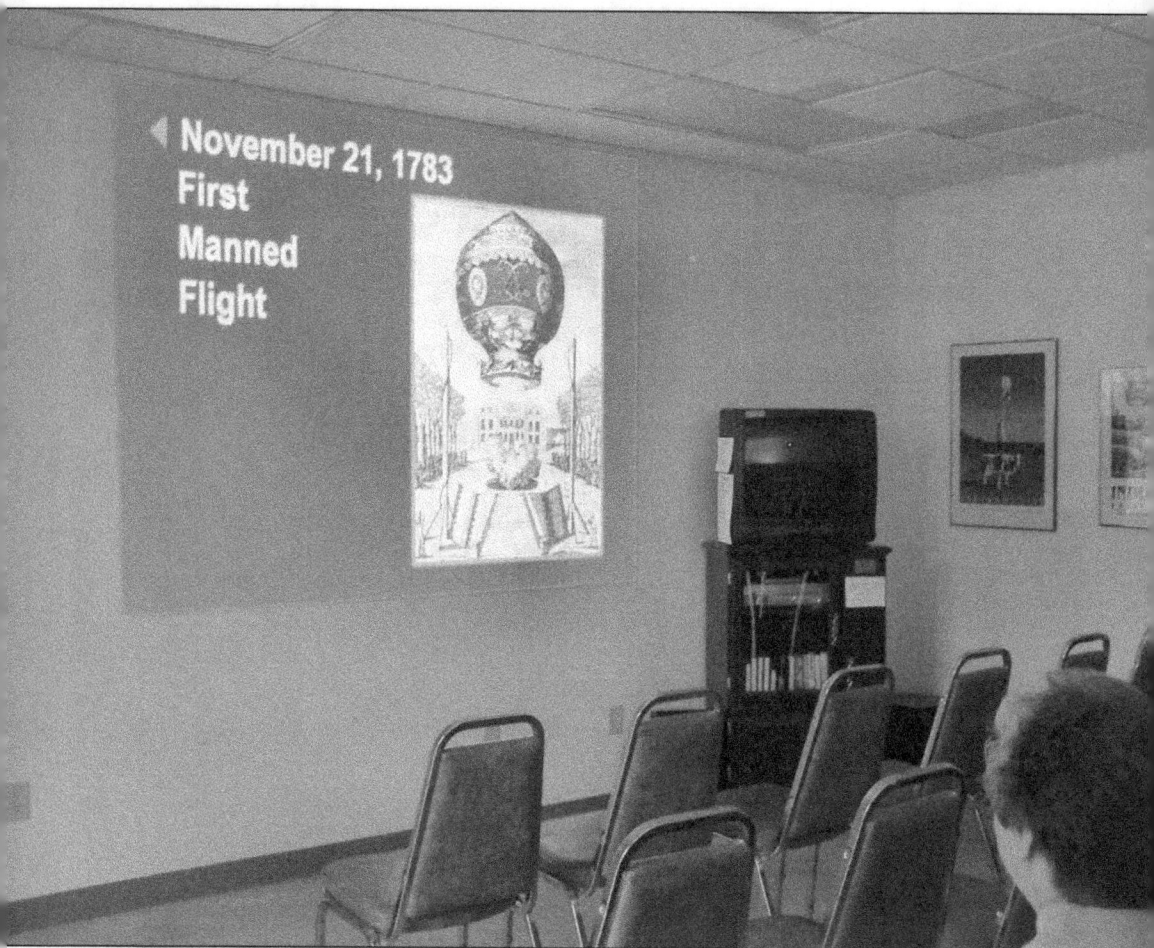

The museum theater, where patrons can view slide shows or videos about ballooning, seats up to 25 persons. The most-viewed show is a 20-minute slide show with narration entitled "A Short History of Ballooning," which tells an overview of the history of ballooning from its beginning in 1783 to the present. Other shows include the following: "A Trip to the Hot Air Balloon Festival" for children; the "Channel Champ," the first hot air balloon to cross the English Channel in 1963; "Lighter Than Air," a history of ballooning by ReMax; the "National Balloon Museum," an illustrated history of the museum; and "Balloons Over Indianola," a photograph album. (Photograph by and courtesy of Dennis D. Nicholson.)

One of the first items one sees when entering the museum is this exhibit depicting the first time anyone ever flew, in 1783, the story told in chapter two of this book. That exhibit has pictures of the Montgolfier brothers, papermakers by trade, who were the original inventors of the first hot air balloon. It also tells the story of the early test flight with animals and about the connection to the modern air balloon. (Photograph by and courtesy of Dennis D. Nicholson.)

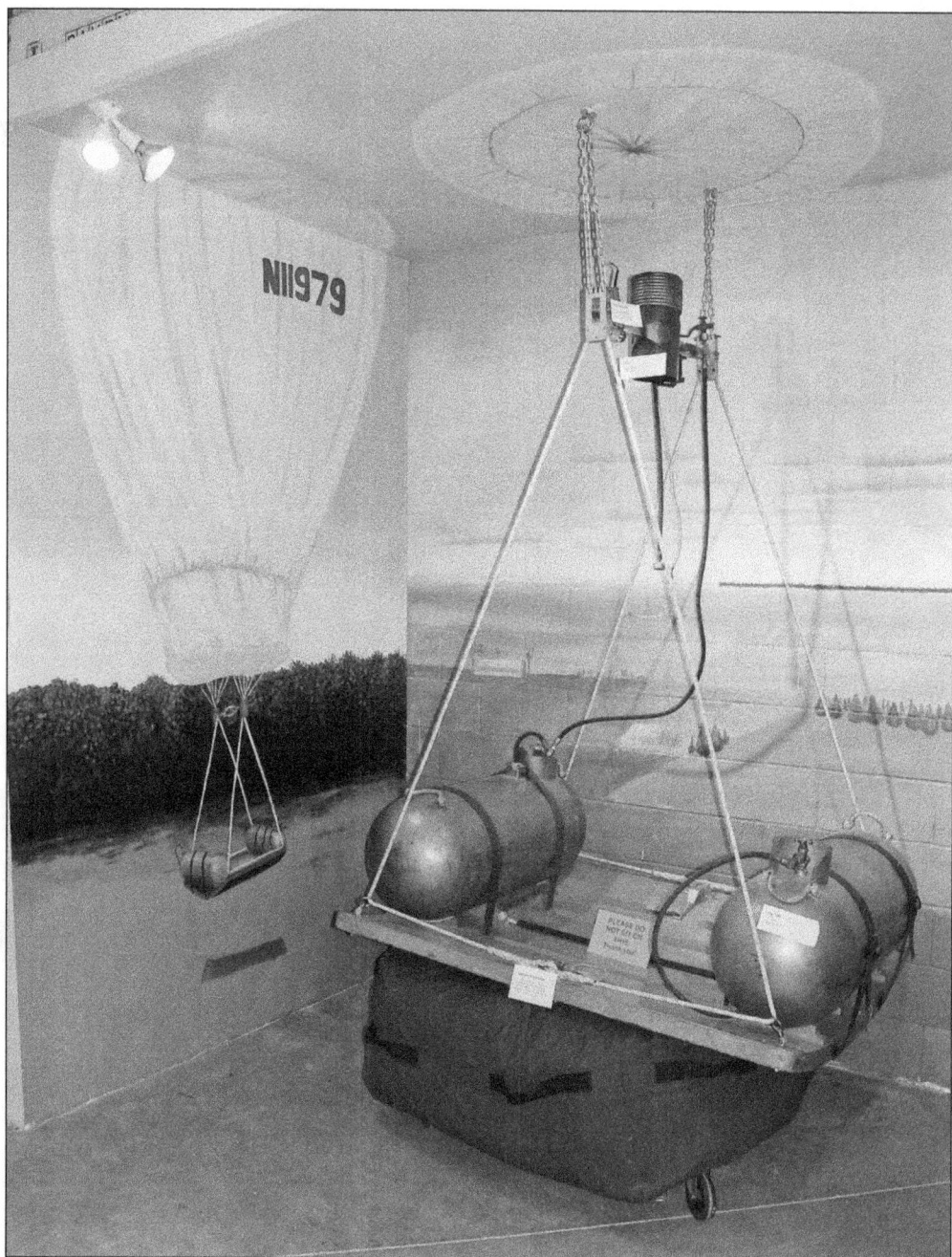

The *Channel Champ* exhibit displays the first hot air balloon to cross the English Channel in 1963. See the full story on pages 30–33. (Photograph by and courtesy of Dennis D. Nicholson.)

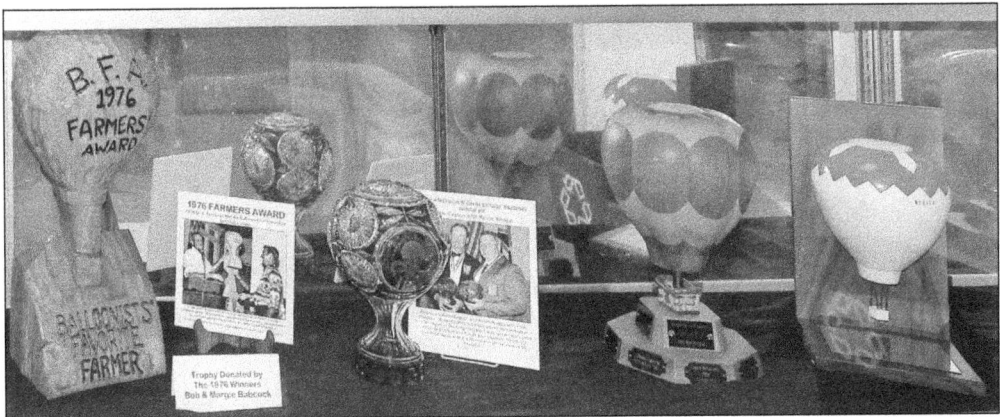

The museum houses a collection of ballooning trophies dating back to 1970 when modern hot air ballooning first started in Indianola. Just five of them are shown on this page. They represent trophies given by balloon clubs, ballooning events, and by the U.S. National Hot Air Balloon Championships. The picture below is of the trophy given to the winner of the U.S. National Hot Air Balloon Championship in 1970. Frank Pritchard from Flint, Michigan, was the recipient. He received 5,340 out of a possible 6,000 points. (Photographs by and courtesy of Dennis D. Nicholson.)

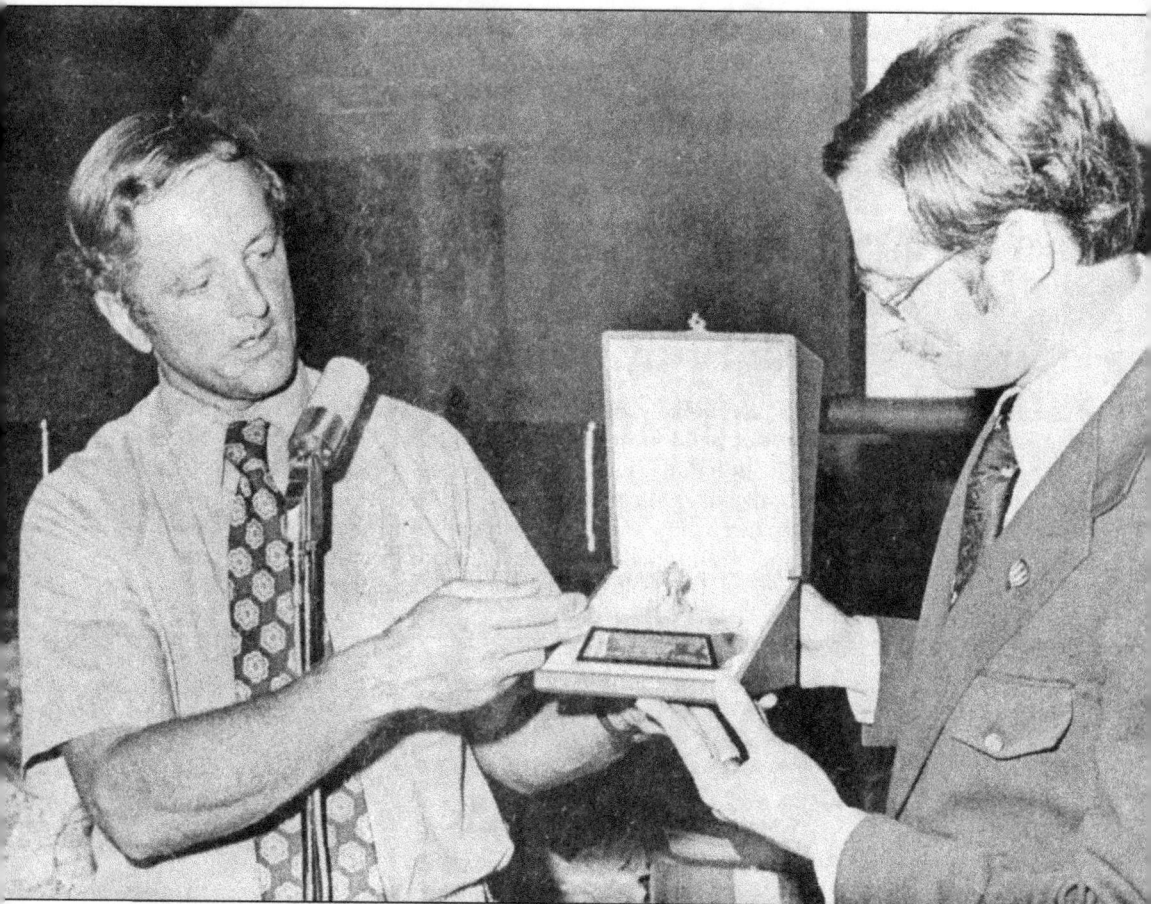

Above, Dr. William Grabb, president of the Balloon Federation of America, presents the 1972 U.S. National Hot Air Balloon Championship trophy to winner Dennis Floden of Michigan. In this year, the trophy was a miniature reproduction of the Jeanette Ridlon Piccard trophy, which is pictured and described in detail on the next page. They also had a brass nameplate placed on the base of the Piccard trophy. That tradition continued for some years, and now each winner receives an etched crystal ice bucket and also has a brass nameplate put on the Piccard trophy. The large trophy always remains in the museum. (Photograph courtesy of the National Balloon Museum Archives.)

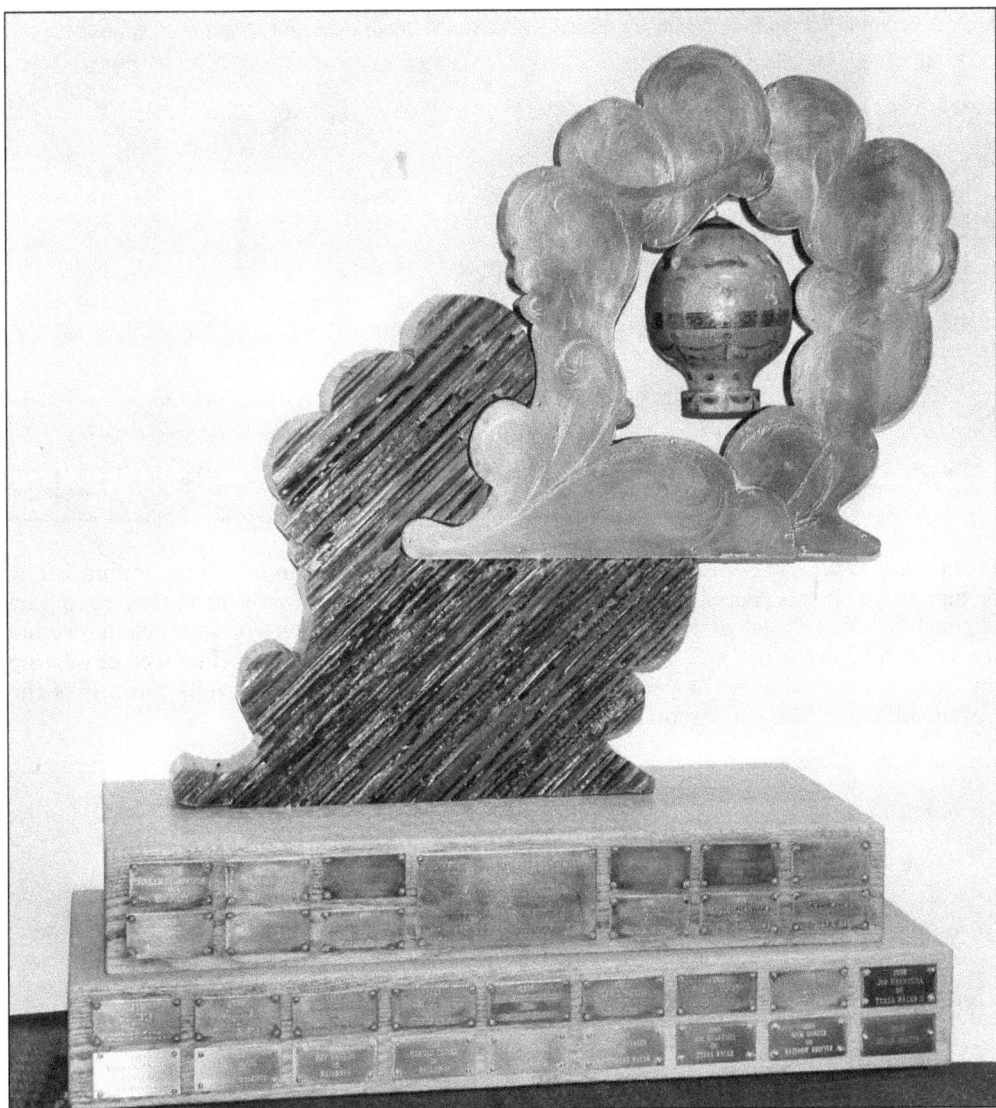

The Jeanette Ridlon Piccard trophy (above) is on permanent display at the National Balloon Museum, but the name of winner of the National Hot Air Balloon Championship is added to the base each year in the form of an engraved brass nameplate. The trophy was presented to the Balloon Federation of America by Don and Willie Piccard. The gold balloon was made by the Belgian goldsmith M. Lotaire. The silver cloud was hand crafted by Sweden's no. 1 licensed balloon pilot, Per Arne Lundahl, who is a goldsmith by profession. The Lucite cloud, or perhaps shadow of the cloud, or maybe even rain cascading from the cloud, was hand laminated by Don Piccard. (Photograph courtesy of the National Balloon Museum Archives.)

In the early 1970s, balloonists and their crew members dressed up in matching uniforms. The picture above on this page shows a museum exhibit of some of the early attire they wore. The picture below shows three of the volunteers for Indianola Balloons, Inc. who were helping operate the ballooning event in 1979. They too had their distinctive jump suits. The idea of wearing uniforms has waned over the years and very few do that now. (Photographs courtesy of the National Balloon Museum Archives.)

The picture above shows the weather exhibit and electronic balloon weather station in the museum. The picture below is the computer screen, which indicates wind speed, wind direction, temperature, humidity, barometric pressure, and other statistics helpful for flying balloons. The computerized weather station is just like the one at the balloon field used by the National Balloon Classic weather advisor to help decide what flight the pilots will take each day. It was donated by the West family. (Photographs by and courtesy of Dennis D. Nicholson.)

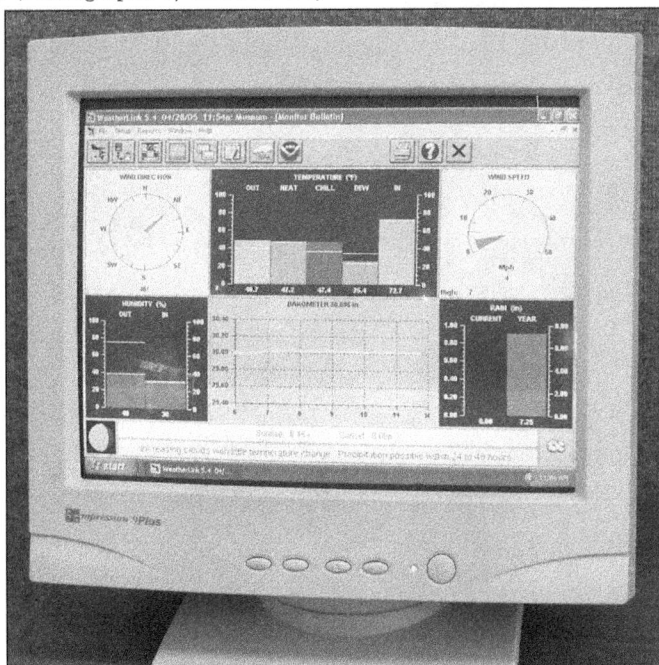

Dr. P. B. West (left), a local dentist and amateur meteorologist, noticed that weather conditions in Indianola were often different from those reported by the National Weather Service at the Des Moines International Airport. He began to use his personal weather instruments to advise the balloonists and soon became the official weather advisor for the Indianola balloon event. He was also the one who started the rural relations committee to work with land owners and balloonists to arrange sites for launching and landing balloons. His son, Dr. Steven West (below left), also a dentist and amateur meteorologist, joined his father, and the two of them worked together until 1986. Steven has more recently been joined by John Holst (below right), an area supervisor for the Federal Aviation Administration in Fort Dodge, Iowa. Steve and John now serve as the weather officials for the National Balloon Classic. (Photographs by and courtesy of Becky Wigeland.)

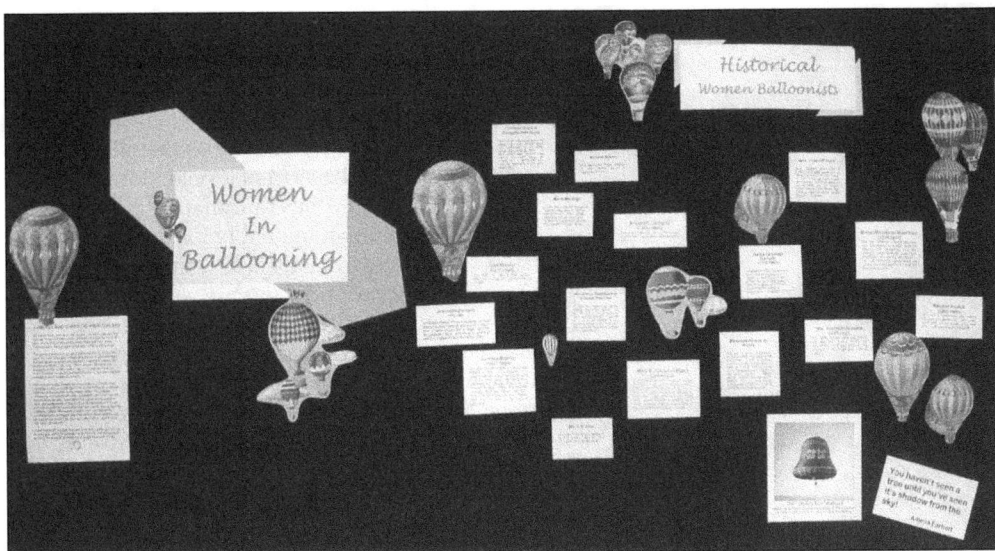

The Women in Ballooning exhibit gives a thumbnail about female balloonists, both living and deceased. There is a large notebook with the exhibit that gives more detailed biographical information, including photographs of the women and their balloon and something about their ballooning careers. Female balloonists may submit their information with a form available on the museum's Web site or request one from the museum. (Photographs by and courtesy of Dennis D. Nicholson.)

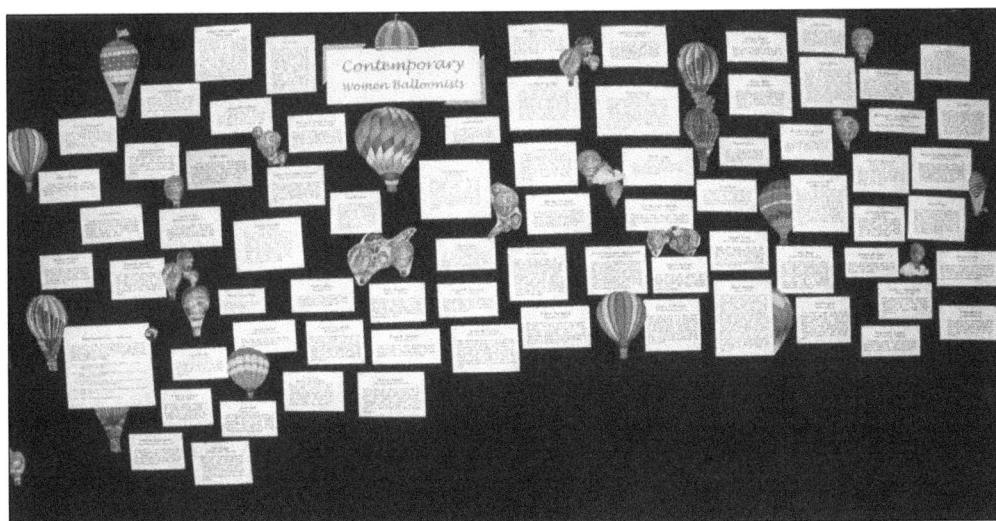

The Women in Ballooning exhibit includes a bronze bust of pioneer balloonist Natalie "Nikki" Caplan given as a memorial by the balloonists of Missouri. She was the first balloon pilot in the state of Missouri. Her first major competition was the 1973 National Hot Air Balloon Championships in Indianola, where she was the only woman to qualify for the finals. She participated in many ballooning events in America, Europe, and Asia. She also piloted a gas balloon in many competitive events. She was active in organizing, teaching, and promoting ballooning and trained many balloon pilots in her state. She served on the Board of Directors of the Balloon Federation of America from 1976–1979. In 1982, she set a new world feminine distance record in a gas balloon in a flight from Albuquerque, New Mexico, to Duncombe, Iowa. In 1983, Nikki received the Montgolfier Diplome, the highest award given by the Federation Aeronautique Internationale. Pictured to the left is her bronze memorial bust, and a photograph of her second hot air balloon, the *Unicorn*, is pictured below. (Left, photograph by and courtesy of Dennis D. Nicholson; below, photograph courtesy of the National Balloon Museum Archives.)

One of the most unusual museum exhibits is the Cameron-made, two-seated gondola of a hot air airship named *St. Louis*. The balloon envelope is shaped like a blimp. The picture above shows the gondola, and the picture below shows the balloon in flight. This was purchased in 1984 by David Rapp from the St. Louis, Missouri, area for $47,000, and he donated it to the museum in 2007. It has the typical 10 million BTU burner and a propeller, which enabled it to fly at a maximum speed of 15 miles per hour, and the aircraft is steerable. (Above, photograph by and courtesy of Dennis D. Nicholson; below, photograph courtesy of David Rapp.)

The museum contains many early gondolas or baskets representing the various manufacturers and the types that have been made. Just a few of them are visible in this photograph. Notable in the picture above is the smoke balloon flown by the famous smoke balloonist Capt. Eddie Allen. His balloon had no burner but was heated on the ground by a smoky fire and was then released and sent aloft. Captain Eddie would parachute down before the crowd. He also had a balloon cannon act where one of his daughters would be "shot" out of the cannon that the balloon took up with it, and they would parachute to the ground. The cannon is shown hanging in the center of this picture. Captain Eddie flew at Indianola a number of times, but the last time, in 1976, his parachute failed to open properly and he was severely injured. That was the last such jump that he made. (Photograph by and courtesy of Dennis D. Nicholson.)

The museum has a gift shop that sells a large variety of ballooning-related items, including t-shirts, socks, mugs, photographs, balloon jewelry, photograph postcards, photograph magnets, tree ornaments, puzzles, books, greeting cards, balloon pins, balloon patches, photograph bookmarks, wind chimes, posters, wind socks, calendars, DVDs, and much more. Some gift shop items are also for sale on the museum Web site. Sales from the gift shop help support the museum's operation costs. (Photograph by and courtesy of Dennis D. Nicholson.)

In 2009, the museum was chosen as one of Iowa's great places in the state's Iowa Great Places program. The program recognizes sites in Iowa with particular appeal and cultural significance. The status as a "great place" makes the museum eligible to apply for state grants for improving the site. In summer 2009, Iowa lieutenant governor Patty Judge (below) visited the museum as a part of her tour of special places in Iowa, presented the Iowa Great Place sign (left), and spoke to a crowd of local area citizens and politicians about how the Great Places program promotes tourism in Iowa. She was also treated to an experience in the basket of a tethered balloon by local balloonist Al Appenzeller. (Photographs by and courtesy of Dennis D. Nicholson.)

The winners of the U.S. National Hot Air Balloon Championships have their pictures posted on the wall with the years they won the event. Some pilots have won several different years. The museum is the official repository for the Balloon Federation of America artifacts. (Photograph by and courtesy of Dennis D. Nicholson.)

The group photographs of the pilots taking part in the National Balloon Classic are posted in the museum. There are generally more than 100 pilots each year. Most compete in the scoring, but some participate just for pleasure flying. (Photograph by and courtesy of Dennis D. Nicholson; original photographs by and courtesy of Tim McConnell Photography.)

Nine

BALLOONING OVER INDIANOLA FASCINATES THE CROWDS

Fascination with colorful balloons still continues to bring thousands of spectators to Indianola each year. Not only are there colorful balloons, but there is musical entertainment before and after flight time. On the 155-acre site, there is also plenty of opportunity for children to run and play, as well as enjoy carnival-type entertainment. There is also time for children and parents to relax and enjoy being together. All of this makes the National Balloon Classic an excellent family event. Hundreds of volunteers are needed to make the event happen.

The National Balloon Classic continues the tradition of the U.S. National Hot Air Balloon Championships begun in Indianola in 1970. During the annual, nine-day event 70,000–90,000 spectators come to view the balloons in flight. They fly early morning and early evening each day, weather permitting. The view above is an early morning flight where the pilots lifted off in the countryside and are attempting to fly into the balloon field and drop their baggies on a target. (Photograph by and courtesy of Dennis D. Nicholson.)

The National Balloon Classic is the second oldest and second largest hot air balloon festival in the United States. It always begins the last Friday of July and runs for nine days. 2010 marks the 41st consecutive year that Indianola has hosted a hot air balloon festival. Typically more than 100 pilots fill the skies over Indianola with their colorful balloons each year. One can even purchase a balloon ride during the classic or possibly get a free ride if one volunteers to crew for a pilot. Shown in the picture above are two ride balloons provided by the On the Fly company from Galena, Illinois. Anyone can buy a ride on one of these during the classic from their red tent, shown in the lower part of the picture. The larger of the two balloons in this picture is a 16-passenger balloon, which has a basket that is divided into five compartments: four for passengers and one in the center for the pilot. (Photograph by and courtesy of Dennis D. Nicholson.)

The classic is a family event with activity opportunities for all ages. People bring their own lawn chairs or rent them at the gate and set up their chairs and/or blankets on the grassy slope in front of the stage and the balloon field. Children can run and play in the wide expanse of grass, or they can try one of the carnival activities shown in the picture. There is even a rubber-wheeled train children can ride in around the grounds. On stage, there is musical entertainment in the late afternoon prior to the flight time. The stage entertainment is repeated following the evening balloon flight as well. (Photograph courtesy of cluster balloonist John Ninomiya.)

Usually two or three nights conclude with a "night glow," where after the balloon flight, the balloons are lined up along the field, and at dusk, the announcer on the public address system in the tower calls on all the pilots to turn their burners on at once. The picture above shows pilots after their evening flight driving back to the field entering on the road from the left and then inflating and lining up their balloons for the night glow. It is tricky to make the balloons glow and keep them cool enough to hold them on the ground. The picture at the bottom shows a small group of balloons glowing. See also the night glow photograph in the color section on page 139. The final night of the classic includes a spectacular fireworks display. (Photographs by and courtesy of Dennis D. Nicholson.)

Both competition and fiesta events are held during the classic. Competitive events are normally held during the morning flights. Usually seven competition flights, each having a varying number of tasks, are held. A task involves flying a balloon toward a target. The wind often goes in different directions at different altitudes, so the pilot can steer toward a target only by changing altitude to take advantage of the wind direction. The target is most often an X or other object on the ground. The pilot drops or throws his baggie toward the target. Score keepers (above) measure the distance each object lands from the center of the target. Those closest to the center get the most points. After competition has ended, the pilot with the most points is the winner. In the photograph above, balloons are trying for the target. The image below shows the scorers from the 1979 National Balloon Classic. (Above, photograph by and courtesy of Dennis D. Nicholson; below, photograph by and courtesy of Thom Roberts.)

The fiesta events are flights normally held in the evening. These flights also test the skill of the pilots, and they can earn prize money, but they are not a part of the competition events for scoring points. They give the balloonmeister a chance to develop different, yet fun tasks for the pilots. These are also designed to be more spectator-friendly types of events. One of the favorite skill contests is the annual Don Kersten Memorial Outhouse Challenge where the balloonists try to fly in and knock over an outhouse, as one lucky balloonist is doing in the photograph above. This event is a friendly reminder of what happened to Iowa's first balloonist, Don Kersten. In 1966, when he was flying at the speedway in Indianapolis, Indiana, his balloon was caught in a sudden wind change, causing his basket to knock over an outhouse, which happened to be occupied by a woman at the time. (Photograph by and courtesy of Ward and Diane Roscoe of mysticmoodsphotography.com.)

Prior to each flight, the pilots meet together with the balloonmeister in a special building called the pilots' compound. The picture above is of one of those meetings. In that meeting, they hear from the classic weather advisors and determine what competition or fiesta event they will perform in the upcoming flight. Should the weather be stormy or the winds too high, they may decide not to fly. Generally speaking, the winds need to be 12 miles per hour or less for ideal flying conditions. The flights are made in early morning and early evening, generally about 6:30 a.m. to 7:00 a.m. or 6:30 p.m. to 7:00 p.m. The reason for that is that the winds are usually calmest at those times of the day. Regulations require the pilots to land by sunset. (Photograph by and courtesy of Ward and Diane Roscoe of mysticmoodsphotography.com.)

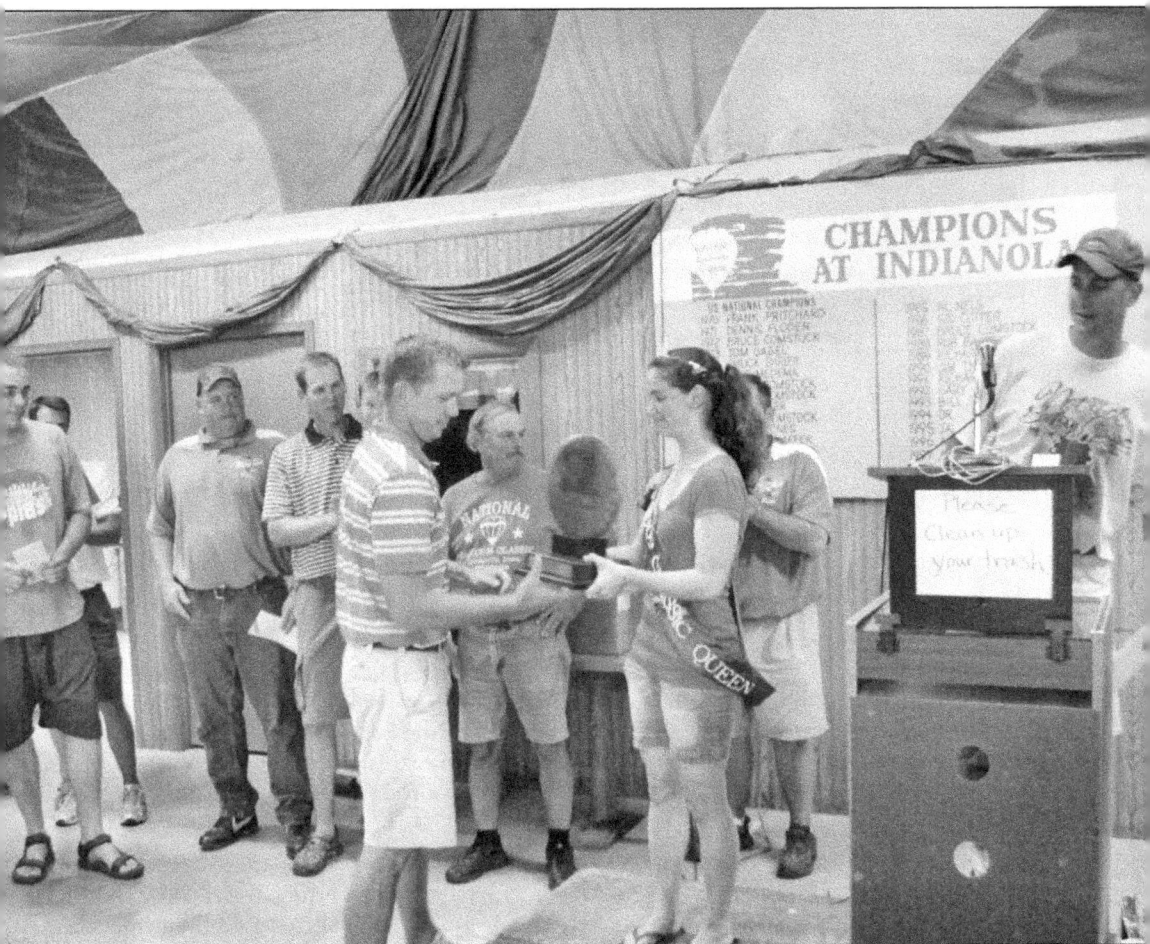

At the end of the nine days of flight, an awards ceremony is held where the pilots receive their awards. They are presented by the National Balloon Classic Queen. The 2009 queen, Jessica Rupp, is shown in the center of the picture as she is presenting the winner's trophy to Jeremy Rubin of Ankeny, Iowa. Dale Crain is standing by the podium, and the others in the picture are other pilots being recognized for their accomplishments. (Photograph by and courtesy of Ward and Diane Roscoe of mysticmoodsphotography.com.)

The National Balloon Classic is held on a 155-acre balloon field east of the city. In the picture above, spectators can be seen in the middle left and in the balloon field (center) with vendors row on the far left. Pilot, crew, and volunteer parking is in the lower left. Visitor parking is just out of view on the left. (Photograph by and courtesy of Ward and Diane Roscoe of mysticmoodsphotography.com.)

The National Balloon Classic has only three paid staff members: a full-time executive director and one part-time staff person in the office, and during the classic, the balloonmeister. Shown above are the current staff, consisting of Becky Kakac, secretary, and Greg Marchant, executive director. Previous directors include Jim Madson, Jerry Harmison, Paddy Kalahar, Gary Ruble, Marlene Wall, Judy Porter, Christy Wildung, Chris Gooddale, Gerald Knoll, and Hilleary Lockhard. Bill Clemons of Des Moines is the current balloonmeister. Otherwise, the classic is a huge volunteer effort requiring 700–900 volunteers to make the event happen. (Photograph by and courtesy of Dennis D. Nicholson.)

The volunteers are divided into nine major categories: public information, parking (which is handled by the local rotary club), gate attendants for three gates, crew recruitment, launch directors, rural relations, pilot relations, scoring, and security. Shown above is launch director Mark Ziino (standing) with Arlan Brown, longtime volunteer crew coordinator. (Photograph by and courtesy of Dennis D. Nicholson.)

The classic is funded through one presenting sponsor, about 120 corporate or individual sponsors, by memberships, an annual fund-raiser, by vendor fees, gift shop sales, pilot registration fees, and spectator admission fees. Above is a view of the vendors row with spectators in the foreground. More details about the classic are available at www.nationalballoonclassic.com. (Photograph by and courtesy of Dennis D. Nicholson.)

The National Balloon Classic Board of Directors sets policies and does much volunteer work for the event including grounds maintenance, cleanup, and a host of other jobs. Pictured above are members of the 2010 board. They are, from left to right, (seated) Mark Clark, Al Appenzeller, Ken Beane, and Tom Comfort; (standing) Cory Frank, Rich Whisler, Heather Palmer, Nate Fehl, and Drew Bracken. Members not present for the picture are Dale Crain, Darcy Moeller, Kerry McKasson, Roger Overman, Rich Nelson, and Charlie Nelson. Other support is provided by the Warren County Sheriff's Department for traffic control, Indianola-Mercy Jefferson Medical Clinic first aid station, Indianola Fire Department and ambulance service, and by approximately 17 food vendors. (Photograph by and courtesy of Dennis D. Nicholson.)

The Iowa balloon, pictured in 1973, carries the design and colors of the Iowa flag. The Iowa balloon was owned first by Steve Kersten and later by Dave Beukelman, both of Fort Dodge, Iowa. The envelope of this balloon is on exhibit in the National Balloon Museum. (Photograph by and courtesy of Dick Stamberg.)

A colorful launch at Simpson College is pictured here in the 1970s. (Photograph by and courtesy of Thom Roberts.)

Pictured on the left is the *Loonar Magic*, owned by Gary Fouche and Jacob Hermanson. On the right is *Simplicity's Charm*, the Simpson College Balloon, in 1978 (Left, photograph by and courtesy of Ward and Diane Roscoe of mysticmoodsphotography.com; right, photograph courtesy of the National Balloon Museum Archives.)

Don Kersten flies his *Merope* balloon carrying the Papal Flag during the 1979 visit of Pope John Paul II to Living History Farms in Des Moines. (Photograph courtesy of the Don Kersten family.)

This is a photograph of an early morning flight of balloons coming toward the balloon field in 2007. (Photograph by and courtesy of Dennis D. Nicholson.)

On the first Saturday morning of the balloon event each year, there is always a parade in downtown Indianola. This photograph is of the parade marshal's car in the parade of 1970. Dale Hicks is seated on left and Don Kersten is seated on the right. Gary Ruble is driving. (Photograph courtesy of the National Balloon Museum Archives.)

Balloons are inflating on the Simpson College field in the 1970s. (Photograph by and courtesy of Thom Roberts.)

This view from 1978 shows, from left to right, the *Bruiser* piloted by Jim Humes of Fort Dodge, Iowa; *Astra* piloted by Father Lawrence Burns of Des Moines and Gary Ruble of Indianola; *Fantasia* piloted by James V. Neill of Riverwoods, Illinois; and the *Blue Max* flown by Jeff Thompson of Des Moines, Iowa. (Photograph courtesy of the National Balloon Museum Archives.)

Pictured here is *Luck of the Irish* in 1979. It was owned by Jerry and Becky Riley. (Photograph by and courtesy of Thom Roberts.)

In this 1983 view of balloons reflected in a pond, the balloonists are waiting for their chase crews to get landowner permission in order to come and retrieve them from the field. (Photograph by and courtesy of Thom Roberts.)

Balloons aiming for the target, with scorers on the ground, are seen in this photograph. The red and yellow one has landed. (Photograph by and courtesy of Ward and Diane Roscoe of mysticmoodsphotography.com.)

This is a morning flight over Indianola in 2005. (Photograph by and courtesy of Dennis D. Nicholson.)

The red, white, and gold balloon above is *Under the Big Top*, flown here by Tim McConnell of Indianola at the 2007 classic. He is often the first one to launch, and the other balloonists watch him to see where the wind is going. (Photograph by and courtesy of Dennis D. Nicholson.)

A mass ascension is getting underway on the National Balloon Classic balloon field. The target "X" is clearly visible in the lower right corner of the field, used in competition. (Photograph by and courtesy of Ward and Diane Roscoe of mysticmoodsphotography.com.)

This photograph shows a mass ascension in 2006. The balloon in the center carries the banner of the Community State Bank of Indianola, Norwalk, and Lucas, which has been the main sponsor of the classic for several years. (Photograph by and courtesy of Dennis D. Nicholson.)

Included in the picture above are two racing balloons. They are the two shaped like a football. From left to right are *Jack's UpSky* piloted by Ken Walter from Waukesha, Wisconsin; *Phoenix Son* piloted by Scott Allsup from Tempe, Arizona; *Conquistador* piloted by Gary Haynes from Indianola; and *Last Lap* piloted by Ron Nollen from Hartland, Wisconsin. (Photograph by and courtesy of Dennis D. Nicholson.)

This photograph shows an early morning flight on a calm day in 2007. (Photograph by and courtesy of Dennis D. Nicholson.)

This scene is a typical night glow showing the pilots all lighting their burners at the same time at dusk. (See story about night glow on page 121.) (Photograph by and courtesy of Dennis D. Nicholson.)

This is the National Balloon Museum building and its Jill Rubin Memorial 2000 window. In October 2000, Jill Rubin, one of Indianola's local balloon pilots, a member of the museum board of directors and museum volunteer, died suddenly while attending the Albuquerque International Balloon Fiesta. Using funds donated in her memory, Indianola artist Grant Dyer was commissioned by the museum to design and create a round, 6-foot stained glass window for the museum as a memorial to Jill. The window displays the two balloons she owned (the two largest ones) along with others and the city water tower located adjacent to Simpson College where ballooning in Indianola began. The ballooning activity in Indianola and the presence of the National Balloon Museum here have made the city both the ballooning capital of Iowa and the primary repository of ballooning history for the nation. (Photographs by and courtesy of Dennis D. Nicholson.)

Arky has 26 inflated animals, one for each letter of the alphabet with each of the seven continents represented. Note its large size compared to two regular balloons. (Photograph by and courtesy of Dennis D. Nicholson.)

The *Purple People Eater* balloon is always a crowd-pleaser. It is flown by John Cavin of Menlo, Georgia. (Photograph by and courtesy of Dennis D. Nicholson.)

This is a cluster balloon flown by John Ninomiya at the 2009 National Balloon Classic. (Above, photograph by and courtesy of Dennis D. Nicholson; below, photograph by and courtesy of Ward and Diane Roscoe of mysticmoodsphotography.com.)

A balloon is shown over a railroad near Indianola in 1971. When you are ballooning, you are always on the right track. (Photograph by and courtesy of Thom Roberts.)

Visit us at
arcadiapublishing.com

www.ingramcontent.com/pod-product-compliance
Lightning Source LLC
Chambersburg PA
CBHW080544110426
42813CB00006B/1209